AND OUR
DEFENSE
IS SURE

Editorial Committee

Chaplain, Colonel, Harmon D. Moore, Chairman
Headquarters, Military District of Washington
United States Army

Captain Ernest A. Ham, Chaplain, Vice Chairman
Headquarters, Potomac River Naval Command
United States Navy

Chaplain, Lieutenant Colonel, Clarence E. Hobgood, Secretary
Headquarters Command
United States Air Force

Edited by
HARMON D. MOORE

ERNEST A. HAM

CLARENCE E. HOBGOOD

Sermons and Addresses from the
Pentagon Protestant Pulpit

AND OUR
DEFENSE
IS SURE

ABINGDON PRESS
NEW YORK
NASHVILLE

AND OUR DEFENSE IS SURE

Copyright © 1964 by Abingdon Press

Library of Congress Catalog Card Number: 64-14618

Scripture quotations designated RSV are from the
Revised Standard Version of the Bible, copyrighted
1946 and 1952 by the Division of Christian Education, National Council of Churches, and are
used by permission.

Scripture quotations designated NEB are from
The New English Bible: New Testament. ©
The Delegates of the Oxford University Press
and the Syndics of the Cambridge University
Press, 1961. Used by permission.

SET UP, PRINTED, AND BOUND BY THE
PARTHENON PRESS, AT NASHVILLE,
TENNESSEE, UNITED STATES OF AMERICA

To Our Men and Women in the Armed Forces
Who in
War and Peace
Strive to Make OUR DEFENSE SURE

PREFACE

The Pentagon Protestant Pulpit is the outgrowth of occasional weekday noon-hour services conducted by chaplains in the Concourse of the Pentagon. The purpose of this program was to make vivid to our defense forces the great cultural and religious heritage which undergirds our nation. The Pulpit now operates under a committee of chaplains of the Army, Navy, and Air Force. Outstanding Christian leaders have responded to the Pulpit's invitation to speak there and have consented to the publication of what they had to say.

Here are words "so vascular and alive they would bleed if you cut them." They were spoken from a free pulpit at the nerve center of the free world's defenses, and they have a potency of life as active as the spirits of the men who proclaimed them. The speakers came to say their piece in the presence of the people, military and civilian, who carry the burden of decision amid tensions in which gigantic powers struggle for huge stakes. If you do not know this audience, you can brush them off with trite, made-to-order expressions—such as arbitrary, power thirsty, news managers, or even "the brass"—but not so if you really know them and deeply care about the ramparts of freedom. To speak to them in words that are medicine for the soul calls for supremest dedication of choicest spirits. No other words will do. The best thought of the Church is their due. Men who have a name for knowing what America should do have spoken, and continue to speak in this free pulpit. This volume goes forth in the belief that some of what has been said should reach a wider audience, for here are recorded the essence and quintessence of men's lives, the reasons why men work and sacrifice and even dare to die. The reward that is offered, like the goal that is sought, is liberty and justice for all mankind "amid the flood of mortal ills prevailing."

Following each address the chaplains invited the speaker and representative leaders of the three services and the Defense Department to a luncheon at which an opportunity was given for individuals to ask questions and where a more intimate and informal discussion ensued.

The editors wish to offer sincerest thanks to the contributors who have generously contributed their work on request to the creation of this volume. We also wish to express our appreciation to Chaplain William L. S. Keen for his assistance in editing three of the manuscripts; to Robert S. Loiselle, Patricia McKnett, and Sandra Pearce for typing the entire manuscript; and to Violet N. Breeding and Lehman F. Cheshire for many hours of editorial assistance and support.

CONTENTS

Youth Wants a Cause

E. STANLEY JONES

☆☆☆ What can we give to youth? What is its greatest need? If I were to give youth one thing, I think I would choose a cause. A professor of Harvard University, speaking over the radio, said, "The health of this country is being undermined by purposelessness." We've got to have a cause. So I'm going to suggest that we give youth a cause —perhaps two causes. One with a small c, the other with a capital C. One taken from the history of our country, the other taken from our Scripture.

All through our national life we have been fighting about a word. It's the word "all." Found in our Declaration of Independence—"all men are created equal." Found in our Pledge of Allegiance to the flag—"with liberty and justice for all." We've tried to make the *all* into *some*. It refuses to remain some, however, and demands that all be all. That word "all" has precipitated eight great crises in our national life.

The first evolved around whether we would make the territories surrounding the original colonies equal with the original colonies or not. The alternate pattern was empire. We came near taking it. When we were about to take in the people of the Ohio Valley, Timothy Dwight, the president of Yale University, asked, "Are you going to take in the people of the Ohio Valley, make them equal? They are incapable of civilization, cultural or religious, too talkative, and won't pay their debts." But we took in Ohio, and Ohio has given more Presidents to the United States than all New England from which Dr. Dwight spoke so loftily. When we were about to take in Missouri, Josiah Quincy stood up on the floor of Congress and said, "Are you going to pour upon the floors of this Congress the wild men of Missouri to settle the affairs of the Seaboard fifteen hundred miles away from their native haunts?" But we took in Missouri. When we were about to take in the land west of the Rockies, a representative of Missouri, of all places, said, "I suggest that a monument be placed upon the Rocky Mountains to the God Terminus, the end! There's nothing beyond the Rocky Mountains except sagebrush and cactus—nothing that anybody wants." Tell that to California, Washington, Oregon! Everytime we took a fresh new territory to make it equal we did it with a great deal of searching of heart and fear that democracy was in danger. But we found to our glad surprise that when we extended the word "all" to all we came to stability. For the wounds of democracy could only be healed by further democracy. We became a republic instead of an empire by the extension of the word "all" to all.

The second place where we fought with that word "all" was over the question whether we would apply it to the people of all faiths. It comes as a shock to remember that we hanged Quakers in the New England colony just because they were Quakers. And then comes another scene: A man, the chosen representative of the American people, walks up the steps to the White House. It is Herbert Hoover, a Quaker. That measures the length that we have gone in applying that "all" to people of all faiths. We decided that we want a civilization in which everybody has a right to worship God or not to worship God according to the dictates of his conscience.

The third place where we struggled with this word "all" was over the question whether we would apply it to women. We took seriously the statement that "all men are created equal." We were not sure about the women. We kept them out of our professions, out of our universities, and gave them the right to vote only in 1922. And we are still struggling over the question of equal pay for equal work. Benjamin Kidd, the sociologist, said that "women are to be the psychic center of power in the future." What did he mean by that? He also said the future belongs to co-operation; across it is written co-operate or perish. Women, when true to their function, represent the co-operative order. It is theirs to make out of diverse and conflicting elements in the home a co-operative order. Man on the other hand represents competition; he must compete with his brother and nature to gain a living. The future, said Kidd, belongs to co-operation. Then women, if true to their function, are going to be the psychic center of power. They are going to give the spirit which is going to mold that co-operative order—a high destiny and not one to be sniffed at. They tell me that the women now hold 75 per cent of the wealth of this country in their hands. And then they tell me that the women now do 90 per cent of the purchasing. The group that will be the psychic center of power in a co-operative future and that holds 75 per cent of the wealth and does 90 per cent of the purchasing then has a destiny, perhaps a decisive destiny. But a great many of the women seem bent upon being as much like the men as possible. My advice to them is this: If you think you are going to get us by being like us, you've missed the bus. You had better stay on your pedestals and be different.

The next place where we struggled with that word "all" is over the question: Do we apply it to the child? The woman and the child were the weaker members of society, and they came into their rights last. Jesus set the child "in the midst." Of whom? Everybody, and said that if anyone hurts the mind, the soul, the body of a little child "it would be better for him if a great millstone were hung round his neck and he were thrown into the sea." We have hurt the soul, the mind, the body of a little child. And our civilization is still doing it. They tell me that 95 per cent of the delinquents come out of broken homes. The Chinese say, "In a broken nest there are no whole eggs." The security of the home is broken up and the child turns delinquent. The sag then has not been as much in youth as it has been in the older age, my generation. The older generation wouldn't live with God, now they can't live with one another. And if you won't live with God, you can't live with yourself.

And if you can't live with yourself, you can't live with anybody else. Yes, the sag is in the older generation.

I said in a meeting sometime ago, "There's nothing wrong with this younger generation except the older." A little fellow, about twelve, piped up and said, "Say, you've said something!" The sag, I repeat, is in the older generation.

The next place where we struggle with that word "all" is over the question whether we would apply it to labor. This has been a conflict in our civilization all down through the ages—this conflict between Hamiltonism and Jeffersonism, between capital and labor, between property and people. I'm persuaded that we will never have stability in this country if capital conquers labor—or if labor conquers capital. Both must change and come to a third position, gathering up the truth in capital, the truth in labor into a third something—what Paul calls a "new man." What would a new man out of both parties in industry mean? It would mean, I believe, a labor-capital management and a division of the profits and losses. A new man out of both parties. I said that to the Chicago Rotary, and when I got back to my hotel I had a call from an official of The First National Bank, who said, "We were very interested in what you said about putting profit sharing in industry. You might be interested to know that as a bank, whenever we take over an industry to finance it, the first thing we try to get them to do is to put in profit sharing. We don't do it because of charity but because it makes for better business, better relationships, and more production."

The next place where we have struggled with the word "all" is over the question whether we would apply it to the man of color. We have said that the Negro could stay in our civilization provided he stayed subordinate, in his place. I love this Pledge of Allegiance to the flag. Something goes up and down my spine everytime I hear those words, "with liberty and justice for all." But once my blood ran cold. It was in a Negro school. I said to the teacher, "How can your young people say 'with liberty and justice for all?' " I knew how they were discriminated against. She said, "You know how they say it? Under their breaths they add two words, 'with liberty and justice for all, but me!' " A nation that makes a part of its citizenry say that under its breath is denying the fundamental basis upon which that nation is built. We can do one of two things; either change the pledge and say "with liberty and justice for some," and in brackets put "white people," in which case democracy is gone and racialism has been substituted and Hitler has won; or we can change our attitudes and say "with liberty and justice for all" and mean the all, apart from race and birth and color and sex and religion. What's happening in our country is a part of a world revolution. The underprivileged are on the march. This has the ground swell of a world revolution behind it. The upsurge of a social revolution. I welcome it. A Negro minister put it this way, "The bell is tolling, the tide is roaring in, you can no more stop it than you can turn back the tides of Hampton Roads with your two hands." And nobody of goodwill wants to stop it.

The next place where we have struggled with that word "all" is over the question whether we would apply it to people of Asiatic origin. We took American citizens, Japanese-Americans (note the word citizens), when the war came on and we put them behind barbed wires, without trial, without charge. Yet in many ways they were one of the finest groups in our national life. They had more young people in college than any other racial group, less crime percentage against them, almost none of them on relief. And more of their young people were in the American army than any other racial group, eighteen thousand. They were the most decorated portion of the American army. They won over one thousand purple hearts, had not one desertion, not one AWOL. I'm proud of them, and grateful for the contributions they have made and are making.

The last place that we've struggled over that word is over the question whether we would apply "all" to everybody at home and then to others abroad. Some people think that the next century is going to be the American Century. We will be different, benevolent, but we will be dominant. If we go out to dominate anybody economically, socially, politically, militarily our name will be mud! That would be the saddest ending to the greatest beginning in human history, for we who began by breaking off from empire would end up by setting up an empire of our own, and angels would weep. It's not our business to dominate anybody. Then what is our business? We've been entrusted with a word "all." We should apply that word "all" to everyone at home and then go out and make our foreign policy that Pledge of Allegiance to the flag "with liberty and justice for all." And if we do that, the Communists won't have a look in. For they can only operate where there are ghastly inequalities.

What then is the first thing that we would entrust to youth? The thing that we as a nation have been entrusted with: We've been trusted with the word "all." We haven't done too well with it but we've done better than any other nation. We have struggled with it. It's going to win for it is right. So I say to youth, take that word "all," apply it to all at home, and then go out "with liberty and justice for all." The future is in the hands of those who apply the word "all" to all. This is the cause I would entrust. And if they accept it, the youth of our day can become invincible, because the future belongs to those who make "all" all. The only way to beat the Communists is to beat them to it. That's the cause, the first cause I would entrust.

The second is this. And this is the cause with the capital C. I was in Russia. It hit me hard. I saw them building up a civilization without God, and doing it enthusiastically. Coming out of the subways carrying earth, the young men would chant, "We're making a new world, we're making a new world." They felt they were. I was shaken. I went to my Bible one morning in Moscow and a verse arose out of the Scripture, spoke to my condition, as the Quakers would say. This verse, "Let us be grateful for receiving a kingdom that cannot be shaken." (RSV.) I said to myself, Have we got an unshakeable kingdom? The kingdom of God? In the midst of a shaken world have we got an unshakeable kingdom? And everything within me said yes.

The next morning I came back again and another verse arose out of the Scripture and spoke to my condition, this one a few verses below. "Jesus Christ is the same yesterday and today and for ever." (RSV.) I said to myself, have we got an unchanging person? And the answer, "Yes." "Change and decay all around I see," but there's One that doesn't change—the same yesterday, today, and forever—the Son of God.

I came out of Russia with two things in my mind and heart. An unshakeable kingdom and the unchanging Person. They were two then, now they have coalesced and become one. I see that this unshakeable

18

order is embodied in an unchanging person, the Absolute Order and the Absolute Person coincide. Is that our message, is that our cause?

Out of the Scripture comes this word: "Seek ye first the kingdom of God . . . and all these things shall be added unto you." "All these things shall be added unto you!" Get your central loyalty straight. I've given you the cause of "all," small c. And now I am giving a cause with a capital C, "Seek ye first the kingdom of God." "And all these things," including our liberties, will be "added unto you."

One word more. A doctor told me he had been called in by a patient having very severe attacks of asthma. He couldn't find any basis for these attacks, and so he said to this man, "Is there something troubling you?" And the man said, "No, doctor. I'm a member of the church; I'm an official in the church." So the doctor went away puzzled. But the next day this patient sent for him and said, "Doctor, I've been thinking all night about what you said; I haven't slept; I've been in prayer. I looked up at this ceiling and I saw the words in bright letters, 'Seek ye first the kingdom of God.' I looked up on the wall and those letters were there! 'Seek ye first the kingdom of God.' I looked at the floor and those bright letters were there, 'Seek ye first the kingdom of God.' Doctor, I have not been seeking first the kingdom of God. I've been seeking first the kingdom of John Brown. (That wasn't his name but we will use it.) I have risen to the top in my corporation, climbed careless of what happened to anybody else. I sought my own kingdom. I arrived at the top, but I did it for myself. Now, doctor, something happened to me during the night. I'm going to 'seek . . . first the kingdom of God.' I don't know what's going to happen to my asthma, but now I'm a happy man. I've got something to which I can give my life, 'the kingdom of God.'" And when he did that everything fell into place. For when you seek God's cause first and foremost then these lesser things take their places.

What shall we give to youth? A cause, the word "all"; I'd like to see them take it and go out and make "all" mean all to everybody everywhere—"liberty and justice for all." Then I'd like to see them give their loyalty to the supreme cause, the kingdom of God—the order that cannot be shaken in the midst of a shaken world. There is one unshakeable kingdom, only one. The kingdom of self is shakeable; the kingdom of health is shakeable; the kingdom of property is shakeable; the kingdom of nationalism is shakeable; every kingdom in this world is shakeable at least by death. But there is one unshakeable kingdom and if youth will say, "All right, that's our cause with a capital C," then all these things, including the future, will be given to them.

And to these two great things I dedicate youth in your name, my name, our name. And with youth we ourselves must practice them; and if we go out with this lesser cause and this greater cause, then the future is secure. I don't know what the future holds, but I know *who* holds the future. If we ally ourselves with him we ally ourselves to that future.

The Nature of Our Warfare

CYRIL BLACK

☆ ☆ ☆ The apostle Paul spoke these words to the Ephesians concerning the warfare in which the Christian is engaged: "For we wrestle not against flesh and blood, but against principalities, against powers, against the rulers of the darkness of this world, against spiritual wickedness in high places." (Eph. 6:12.)

The name Pentagon is known today throughout the world. In some parts of the world it is heard with confidence and in other parts with fear. It brings confidence to those nations who are contending alongside with us for freedom and decency in this twentieth-century world, and it brings fear to those who are the upholders of tyranny and who deny the spiritual factors in which we believe and for which we contend.

Your great republic and my country have been companions in arms in two global wars, and on both occasions our conflict has been against the cruel forces of tyranny. We have shouldered arms together in the fight for democracy and freedom and human decency.

It is unhappily true of the whole story of mankind that history is the record of wars and of rumors of war, and today we live in an age in which war has been classified under two heads—the cold war and the hot war. The nature of the conflict in this year is different from the nature of previous conflicts. The conflict against which we make our preparations today is not so much the conflict of outward things of armies or armaments, of strategy or tactics, of all the vast paraphernalia of modern warfare. The conflict for which we prepare is much more a matter of the heart and the mind. Whether we understand or not the nature of the conflict will very largely determine its outcome—whether we shall be victorious or be vanquished.

Multitudes of our people who dwell in America, in Britain, in Europe, in other parts of the free world do not fully comprehend the nature of the conflict that confronts mankind today. It is not a conflict in the sense of so many wars of earlier times. It is not primarily concerned with national boundaries, with world trading interests, with colonial territories or with any matters of this kind. The dangerous ignorance of multitudes of our people about the true inwardness of the conflict is a source of danger to the nations of the free world.

The Bible says, "If the trumpet gives an uncertain sound, who shall prepare himself for the battle." We are living in an age in which if the third world war comes the circumstances of the war of 1939-1945 will be magnified many times. In addition to all the horrors of that great global conflict, there will be added, of course, the enormously greater horror that the possibility of the use of nuclear weapons conjures up.

Whether the present conflict remains a cold war or becomes a hot war, basically it is a totally different kind of war from any war in which our nations have formerly taken part. It is a war of ideas, a war of ideologies, a war that can only be won in the hearts and in the minds of men and women. It concerns such fundamental questions as what we believe about man, his destiny, his way of life. Is man the creation of God and immortal, or is he merely a creature living in a world of pagan atheism who has no life beyond the grave? Does man possess of himself, because he has a human personality created by God, certain inalienable rights to worship according to the dictates of his conscience? To live life as seems to his judgment to be right? Or is he merely a pawn in the game of great tyrants and cruel dictators having no rights and no privileges which he can claim for himself?

The issue of the modern conflict will not be primarily settled by the force of arms but by which side has the truest, the strongest, and the purest faith.

The heart of all that I am trying to say is to be found in this simple and basic thought—that we in the free world can only be sure of victory in the solemn warfare in which we are engaged if we and all free peoples have a faith that is stronger and purer and truer than the faith of those who are our opponents.

I want to bear my humble but sincere testimony this morning to my undying conviction that there is only one faith that measures up in the world to this standard, and that is the faith of our Lord and Saviour, Jesus Christ. I believe with all my heart and with all my being that "there is none other name under heaven given among men, whereby we must be saved."

I want to ask you this morning this challenging question: Why is it that the Communists will so often sacrifice so much more for what we believe is a totally mistaken and evil faith than we Christian people are willing to sacrifice for what we know is a true and a noble and an uplifting religion? We are forced to recognize that in the Communist world there are dedicated men and women who are willing to sacrifice all that they are and all that they possess for this new and dynamic faith to which they have committed their whole being, while we Christian people often regard our Christianity as being little more than a superficiality, something that stands right outside our normal everyday living and activities, and that has very little relevance to the problems which confront us day by day. Yet never let us forget that the testimony of the centuries acclaims the supremacy and the uniqueness and the relevance of Jesus Christ to every day and to every age.

Do you remember the moving words Napoleon, that great military leader, when a prisoner on the barren island of St. Helena, spoke toward the end of his earthly life—a life containing on the one hand many glittering triumphs, but on the other many abject failures? When he came to sum up his convictions concerning life and death, he said:

I will tell you who Jesus was. Alexander, Caesar, Charlemagne, and I myself, have founded empires, but upon what do these creations of our genius depend?

Upon force. Jesus has founded His empire upon love, and to this very day millions would die for Him. I think I understand something of human nature, and I tell you that all these men were men, as I am a man. No one else is like Him. Jesus Christ was more than man.

You and I who live in what has been described as "this terrible twentieth century" are in a sense privileged to live in a great period in the world's history—a period in which everything is changing, in which the potentialities of the future are literally unbounded. This is the kind of period of which James Russell Lowell wrote:

> Once to every man and nation comes the moment to decide;
> In the strife of Truth with Falsehood, for the good or evil side;
> Some great cause, God's new Messiah, offering each the bloom or blight,
> .   .   .   .
> And the choice goes by forever 'twixt that darkness and that light.

And that great cause is in a very special sense committed to the responsibility of your nation and mine and to all those nations of the world that stand in the tradition of Christian democracy and Christian freedom. I believe, as I know you believe, that if we are resolute and if we will dedicate ourselves at this tremendously challenging hour, the victory of those great causes in which we believe is assured not only for this generation but for the centuries that lie ahead.

Hearken well to the exhortation of the Apostle. Be sure you take faith as your shield, and let us all take as a matter of personal conviction this profession: It all depends on me, and I depend on God.

Brotherhood

GEORGE E. C. HAYES

☆☆☆ We are constrained to address ourselves to, and to indeed hope for, a universal acceptance of the fatherhood of God and the brotherhood of man. We desire to approach our problems unmindful of the races of man as such—Caucasian, Negro, and the innumerable others indistinguishable by languages or pigmentation of skin—and approach these problems with an eye single to the development and advancement of the human race.

We desire to wholeheartedly accept the challenge with which we ourselves are confronted with an unequivocal answer, "Yes, I am my brother's keeper."

I sincerely hope that, in spite of widely publicized experiences to the contrary, the world at large is becoming more tolerant. Experiences of shame and mortification can be matched by those of love.

I recently had the experience of being on both sides of the wall that separates East and West Germany and saw the full evidence of man's inhumanity to man: forced separation of those bound by ties of blood and loss of life by those attempting to escape from an existence bereft of human dignity and fraught with heartaches and misery. And then in a nearby town that same day, I spent the evening in the company of a group of dedicated young women, under the direction of two older ladies and inspirational leaders, called the Sisterhood of Mary. These young ladies lived and studied in dormitories and classrooms and worshiped in chapels built by their own hands. They assembled and built their own printing press and disseminated Christian literature. Their very presence bespoke love for all mankind, and they lived lives of sacrifice and wholesome worthwhileness in what they expressed as atonement for the great tragedy which the Germans had perpetrated against the Jewish people. Here they were, extending wholehearted welcome to the delegates of International Christian Leadership meeting in Berlin, and by their lives and precepts, exemplifying a boundless love for all mankind. No one could be in their presence for even a few moments without realizing that these were God-fearing people and that this was Christianity at work.

The horrors of the German wall were forgotten in this exemplification of true brotherhood.

I have my own philosophy of brotherhood. It is universal only in that it is individual. As to the ultimate day when all people of the world will respect one another for their real worth without regard to race, creed, or color, I have my misgivings and I know with certainty that no such hoped for cause will be reached in our generation. I am equally sure that you and I can make our contribution and deserve our heavenly reward by daily applying the Golden Rule, by "doing unto others as we would have them do unto us."

I recommend to you this way of life. The best way to accomplish this brotherhood with which we align ourselves is to cleanse our individual souls from hatred and prejudice, to trade tolerance for bigotry, and to put into practice the homely virtues of honesty and truthfulness.

One of the most rewarding experiences of my life is my association for the past seven years with a prayer breakfast group of International Christian Leadership. Every Friday morning a group consisting of a dozen men or more meet at the Federal Trade Building for their breakfast. After breakfast, under revolving assigned leadership or an occasional visiting panelist, we study the Bible and exchange experiences and dedicate and rededicate ourselves as witnesses for Christ. These men are persons of caliber and influence in the community: commissioners; business executives; government officials; judges; former governors; and people who, in their positions, help make the rules and carry out the standards by which this community is governed.

I am surely convinced that these men of various religions, denominations, and types of racial backgrounds make their contributions toward this universal brotherhood to which we aspire. This is one of the practiced groups of lay people now with local, national, and international affiliations which sponsored the President's breakfast here in Washington, participated in by the President of the United States, the Vice President, the President's Cabinet, members of both houses of Congress, and delegates from all over this country; and, at a breakfast that was held here not long ago, representatives from some forty-five foreign countries. This is indeed what we need—leadership under Christ. Brotherhood not forced but spontaneous and voluntary. Brotherhood with which you and I can and should ally ourselves.

It was a great pleasure and opportunity to serve for the National Conference of Christians and Jews held here in Washington. Here again our slogan was Brotherhood.

In these regrettable days, days of wars and rumors of wars; in these hours of growing stress and strain; in the constant struggle in the area of class discrimination, it is refreshing to note that the anomaly of segregation in the armed forces has been successfully abolished. I note with pleasure and quote a few lines from the Department of Defense publication *Integration and the Negro Officer in the Armed Forces of the United States of America.* This publication states that President Truman, in 1946, established a committee charged with the responsibility of examining all existing regulations and practices with a view toward putting into effect, and I quote: "Equality of treatment and opportunity for all persons in the Armed Services, without regard to race, color, religion, or racial origin."

The report of this committee, entitled "Freedom to Serve," was made to the President in 1950 and provided the philosophy and working basis for the program of racial integration with no restriction as to racial quotas, which have advanced with increasing success in the Army, Navy, Air Force, and Marine Corps.

May I share with you the lines of a poem, anonymously written, which I keep on the walls of my home and which is the yardstick by which I attempt to measure my own life and which I recommend to each of you as a way of life designed to bring satisfaction and comfort? It is called "The Man in the Glass."

> When you get what you want in the struggle for self,
> and the world makes you king for a day,
> Just go to a mirror and look at yourself,
> and see what that man has to say.
> For it isn't your father, or mother, or wife,
> whose judgment upon you must pass,
> The fellow whose verdict means most in your life,
> is the man staring back from the glass.
> You may be a Jack Horner, and chisel a plum,
> and think you're a wonderful guy,
> But the man in the glass says you're only a bum,
> if you can't look him straight in the eye.
> He is the fellow to please never mind all the rest,
> for he's with you clear up to the end,
> And you've passed your most dangerous, difficult test,
> if the man in the glass is your friend.
> You may fool the whole world down the pathway of years,
> and get pats on the back as you pass.
> But your final reward will be heartaches and tears,
> if you've cheated the man in the glass.

If we so live that at the close of each day we can look into our mirrors and see a person with no frown of condemnation, I assure you that brotherhood will become the reality for which we all hope and pray.

Do we live up to the heritage of being children of the same Father? As is my custom, I turn for my authority to the Book of books, the Bible. In the second chapter of Malachi, the tenth verse, we find: "Have we not all one father? hath not one God created us?" I accept this language not as a platitude but as a Christian doctrine which may be affirmed emphatically and confidently.

Stock piles for missiles that can strike anywhere on this planet, space travel with all its potentials for destruction, the sweeping away of human practices that even ten years ago would have seemed indestructible: are these things compatible with brotherhood? The answer, of course, is no. Let us not be unmindful, however, that each of us, in his own small corner, can make our contribution so as to merit the divine approval, "Well done, thou good and faithful servant."

Why Faith?

SAMUEL M. SHOEMAKER

☆ ☆ ☆ Ash Wednesday was originally a season of special discipline and preparation for Christian baptism. Later it came to be associated with the remembrance of Jesus' temptations in the wilderness when he went apart to decide how he was going to accomplish his mission.

Why should we set apart a time and give any special attention to faith? Hasn't the time come when faith has gone by? Man is taking things more and more into his own hands. Isn't God getting pushed more and more over to one side? If men can travel through space and create things like hydrogen bombs, isn't God's rule about over and man's begun? And isn't man really God from here on out?

I want to say some things to you this morning about why I believe that faith is and always will be essential.

For one thing, man can't remain among the things that he finds in his world without asking what is the meaning of life itself. I don't know whether you saw an article in *Time* magazine sometime ago which told of a class in philosophy in Warsaw University in Poland where Professor Adam Shaff, the head of the department and a member of the central committee of the Polish Communist Party, was asked by one of his students, "Please don't be angry, but could you explain the meaning of life?" And the professor said he realized that not one but hundreds of students were asking that question and *Time* quotes him as saying, "Communist thinking is ill prepared to deal with these questions."

The asking of a question like that may well frighten Communists more than all the armies of the West. It wasn't a few hundred students who were asking that question with that young fellow, it was all the human race. Once we've gone through with the fascination of science, what science can do, there arises the inevitable and unanswered question, What is it all about? What are we here for? Where did we come from and where are we going? And to those questions science has no answer. Philosophy can guess but that's all it can do. The only answer to questions like that is in God.

Now when you say "God" there very soon arises in your mind a question, yes, but what about evil? How can you square God and the amount of evil in the world? Human suffering has always been in the world—torment of body, torment of mind. It staggers the imagination. The amount of cruelty that men have inflicted on dumb animals and are doing so now, in not only savage countries but also in some scientific laboratories in so-called enlightened countries, is staggering. No wonder Paul said, "The whole creation groaneth and travaileth in pain together until now." You want God to put an end to all evil and all suffering. You say you won't believe in him unless he does. But how do we know what we ask?

Years ago in Oxford there was a professor named C. E. M. Joad who all his life had been a militant unbeliever, because he said he couldn't square the evil in the world with a good God. Later in life he became a Christian and he said it was because he began to see that in order to have character there must be choice, a real choice between real good and real evil. A man made good without his own choice is not a good man, he's a thing. The same God who created this world came into this world himself and lived in it on human terms and redeemed us through his Son, Jesus Christ. He didn't create a static good universe. He created an innocent one with the possibility of choice, evil as well as good, and man chose evil and there was a fall. This exact thing is reproduced in the life of every one of us. Then God provided redemption. That's the Christian view of the world. And it begins to make sense when you believe in God as revealed in Jesus Christ and set out to carry out his redemption into all creation. Faith is never just an attitude. Faith is a kind of warfare. Faith is needed first, I think, to make any sense out of life.

Second, I am convinced that faith is the real origin and basis of human freedom. The war in the world today is between two attitudes toward life. One begins with no God, puts the state above all powers, makes man a puppet of the state, creates tyranny and slavery. The other begins with God, sees man as capable of redemption and finding his highest life in the service of God and his fellows, makes the state an arrangement for co-operation between men in the best interests of everybody.

Many years ago in my church in New York we arranged a series of talks on Christian citizenship. One of the speakers was the late George Sokolsky, not a Christian, a convinced Jew much closer to the Christian outlook than many of us Christians. His column many of us used to read with gratitude for his great wisdom. His theme that night, I shall never forget it, was, "Before you decide what you are going to do, you'd better find out what you believe," and he rang the changes on that for an hour and a half. And after he had dealt with it philosophically, he then dealt with present human affairs in the light of it. It was like an Old Testament prophet standing there in that Christian church talking to us.

The early fathers knew this. William Penn said, "Men must be governed by God or they will be ruled by tyrants." Not long ago Justice Clark of the Supreme Court said, "The founding fathers believed devoutly that there is a God and that the inalienable rights of man are rooted not in the state nor the legislature nor in any other human power but in God alone." Actually the Christian view of human nature lies behind the democratic ideal. Every human soul is infinitely valuable to God. Big or little, young or old, black or white, good or bad, he must be given the right to make his own decisions, with only the limitation that those must not interfere with the freedom and well-being of other people. Faith is the root, and freedom is the fruit. And if you want to enjoy the fruit, you had better look to the root, for that's where it comes from.

You know where I think the greatest danger to America today may be? Not just in communism from without, or even from within, though that danger is ever present. I think it lies in the thousands and millions of Americans who enjoy freedom in this land without knowing where it came from, without having anybody to thank for it. We are today consuming our freedom faster than we are producing it, just as we are doing with our water supply.

How do you produce freedom? By freely obeying God and in no other way that I know. I fear for our freedom when I see so many people who mean by it doing as they please. At base our Western freedom is not freedom to do as you please; it is freedom to obey God as you best understand what God wants you to do. "As we see the right." I was just reading those great words in the Lincoln Memorial a few moments ago.

Now there's only one thing big enough to stand in the way of my own ridiculous selfish little self, and that's God. You may have little interest in faith for your personal needs, but if you've got any interest in which way this country is going for the sake of your children and your descendents—whether it's going toward more godlessness, therefore toward more state interference; or toward faith and therefore more obedience toward God and more control welling up within—then you had better be concerned about the whole Christian enterprise in the world, whether you call yourself a Christian or whatever you call yourself. The great missionaries today are the Communists. When will America wake up to the fact that the only final safety lies in our trust in God, and that means our willingness to live day by day, all of us, just ordinary folk, little folk like us, as nearly as we can in the way God wills and ordains? Faith is needed, I say, if we're going to have any basis for our freedoms, and if we don't want to lose our freedoms.

A third thing faith gives us is the one immovable center which everybody needs if he is going to live adequately and without which we find ourselves split in many pieces and going off in all directions. Whence come the thousands, tens of thousands, that find their way into our mental hospitals? Many are unwanted and unloved, but many more have lost, if they ever had it, any real center for their lives. Unless God is that center, we make the center some other human being or some goal in our work, and if these in any way fail us, where can we turn? People can be a great help and they often are, but in the end they face the same issues we do. Many are so foolish as to think they can handle it all by themselves. And when things are going well we generally can, but what about when grave illness strikes, when financial failure strikes, when we lose someone who means everything to us, when we face death itself? What if bombs began to fall, and these gorgeous buildings in Washington were reduced to dust—it could happen—what then? We listen to these absurd expressions of human optimism, "I am the master of my fate, I am the captain of my soul." What rubbish! What absolute ridiculous egotistical nonsense! We're not here on this earth rich men riding to a sure job in a limousine. We are more like Scott Carpenter when he found himself in the sea 250 miles off course and needing precisely to be rescued. Man is in danger of thinking himself to be Almighty because of his discoveries, but he's going to be the victim of them unless he can control himself. In *Modern Man in Search of a Soul* the great psychologist Carl Jung said: "Among all my patients in the second half of life—that is to say, over 35—there has not been one whose problem in the last resort was not that of finding a religious outlook on life. It is safe to say that every one of them fell ill because he had lost that which the living religions of every age have given to their followers, and none of them has been really healed who did not regain his religious outlook." If life is going to be healthy and happy, you've got to feel back of it some purpose. And if there's a purpose for my life, there's got to be a purpose for the whole business. And that means there's got to be a Purposer, and that means there's got to be God.

The great task, then, is to find a relevant, sensible working faith. That's what we ought to be doing this Lent. Not just going through some pious observances, but really coming into the stream of this thing and finding out what God's about in the world, and how my life can be a footnote to his whole total purpose.

How does this happen? Let me tell you a story about just an ordinary American. In December, 1961, there was a conference called the Pittsburgh Experiment. There was a fellow present from Knoxville, Tennessee. His name is Jim Wolfkiel and he's a photoengraver who works on the Knoxville *News Sentinel*. He was fascinated to hear people talk about what God was doing for them and with them on their daily jobs. He asked questions about it all—how it worked personally and how it worked out with them on the daily job. And after listening to their stories, he said,

"We ought to have a Knoxville Experiment." Jim might have been any-body in this crowd or outside of this crowd, walking through this build-ing. But he went back with a feeling in his heart that he was going to start something if it was the last thing he did.

Now in that particular outfit drinking and gambling were common on the job, so much so that the managers complained to the union. Jim thought if these men could be reached and challenged through small groups, meeting to talk about these matters and pray about them, it might change things. He approached several of them with this same idea. They thought he was a fanatic, wouldn't give him time. He kept on. They had a nice little way in that outfit of dropping type down behind your heels when you go by it if they didn't like you. And if that didn't work, there was one more method and that was to pour a little hot lead in your back pocket. You might not feel it there until you pushed up against a desk or chair or sat down.

Well, Jim kept on for six months; he never gave up. He prayed and he kept trying. And after six months of that, his prayers began to pay off. One of the men came to him and said, "Jim, I've been watching you for six months and anybody who can take what we've been giving you has got something. I was the ring leader of that gang; what have you got? Tell me about it." And that man turned around and began to go the other way and he and Jim started a group. They were slowly joined by other men. He got a group going which now includes every man in the department. Men on night shift meet and pray for two or three minutes every evening before they start work. Each week the group comes to meet an hour before work begins. Recently at a meeting like this the head of the union told how much this group has helped in easing labor-management problems. Not all of their problems were solved, he said, but the climate was different. They had a good beginning toward being solved.

What Jim calls the Knoxville Experiment is only about a year old, but already over two hundred local government and business leaders, educa-tors, clergy, white and blue collar workers are active in it. And next September they plan a city-wide conference with breakfasts and lunches and dinners and seminars. A friend of mine, who has been down there recently, wrote to me and said, "Jim has the complete co-operation of the downtown churches and the backing of the mayor. I have never seen the clergy, government officials, and business executives so excited about anything as they are about this forthcoming conference. It's going to be a real 'wing-ding.' "

Think of one man, single handed, going back into his city, and after a year and a quarter such a result (and Jim has had a heart attack in the meanwhile, by the way, and gotten over it). Is that what America needs? Is that what your home city needs? Is that what Washington needs? Is that your real job this Lent and the rest of your life? You sing that old hymn about "Dare to Be a Daniel." Nobody is going to put us in a lion's pit, but they might just put hot lead in your back pocket. Can you take it? Don't dare to be a Daniel, but I do say, dare to be a Jim.

Let us pray: O God, we thank thee that we live in a land that is so greatly blessed by thee. May we ever hold our liberties as stewards of thy bounty. Deepen in us our faith by helping us more and more to surrender ourselves to thee, and then show us how we may witness, like Jim, by life, by word, to thy power and thy grace. We ask it through Jesus Christ, our Lord. Amen.

How to Handle Guilt

JAMES A. PIKE

✩✩✩ One of the most grave problems of human personalities is how to handle the sense of guilt. It is appropriate at the beginning of Lent that we take a look at this problem from both the physiological and religious points of view. To state the problem in another way, there are two very essential things for a sound human personality and an effective person.

One is an honest sense of self-criticism—the ability to get up over one's self, look at one's self, and assess one's self. The second thing is a healthy sense of self-acceptance—to think one's "OK" in business and ready to go. It is very hard to have both these things at one time, because if we look honestly at ourselves we usually find ourselves unacceptable. We need both, however, because if a man does not have a sense of self-acceptance, he cannot live with himself, and if he doesn't have self-criticism, others cannot live with him. Because there is an apparent conflict between the two objectives, most people settle for self-acceptance and omit the self-criticism. I had a colleague once, to whom I impatiently said: "John, you may be in error but never in doubt." Then, there was a man to whom an acquaintance said, "Joe, do you really think that you have ever been wrong?" Joe said, "Once I was wrong; it was that time I admitted a mistake." Guilt is a great burden. It is the gap between the "ought" and the "is." How do we fill that gap? Since we can't seem to rise to the "ought level," we tend to try to pull the "ought level" down to the level of the "is." That is the usual trick.

For example: "I'm as good as the next fellow, you know." (I may not like him very much, but he is rather useful for this purpose!) Or there is a sort of suburban ethics: "I pay my taxes, mend my fences, don't kick the neighbor's dog, don't butt into other people's business, and don't talk religion. I'm a good guy." This is hardly the biblical norm stated in the ancient *Shamai* which we all know is endorsed by our Lord: "Hear, O Israel, the Lord thy God is one." "Thou shalt love the Lord thy God with all thy heart, and with all thy soul, and with all thy mind."

Another way we work it is to blame it on your past. If we've been of lowly origins we'll say: "You know, I was a dead-end kid." That explains everything. If we've been more sophisticated we say: "Well, you see, my psychiatrist tells me that when I was twelve I had a traumatic experience: My mother glared at me." Or we blame it on somebody else: "If she hadn't said to me what she said to me, I wouldn't have said to her what I said to her." Or we seem to think there is a special exemption of one fault per customer: "I have my faults. The Pikes have always had bad tempers; I have a bad temper; that's just the way I am." Our Lord Jesus Christ said: "Be ye perfect." Not "be ye perfect, except one fault per customer."

And we try to find some great good that came out of the evil: "Well, I certainly gave him a piece of my mind, but it'll do him a world of good!"

I'm sure that everyone could contribute out of his own private collection a number of things which he uses regularly as ways to fill this gap, to make himself feel comfortable with himself. The object of this kind of device (rationalization, defense mechanism, alibi, excuses) is *good*. It is to achieve self-acceptance, and it's absolutely essential that you achieve that. Otherwise you're a hang-dog, you're no good, you're dragging your feet; nobody enjoys you that way. To function well in life you've got to feel OK; you've got to feel you're fine. So the object is good. But the particular method is not good, for two reasons.

First, it desensitizes the sense of self-criticism. You become numb to that and you stay in the same old ruts. You remain offensive to people in the same old ways. Finally your friends or acquaintances write you off in what sounds like a generous comment, but which is the most devastating thing that could be said about a human being. They say: "Well that's just the way Jim Pike is, and that's the way he'll always be." That is to say that Jim Pike is a turnip. But what distinguishes a human being from a rhinoceros or from an apple is *that a human being does not have to be the way he is.* That is the human thing about him; he can look at himself and change himself. I've done it.

Not long ago, I was dressing and by chance looked at myself sideways in a full-length mirror. I found my wife was right in what she'd been saying about me. And, you know, I changed the shape of me. I really did. You may say that's not religion, that's just diet. But diet has a lot to do with religion because God cares what shape we're in. Anyway the illustration shows that a man can look at himself and change himself.

When as to one's moral life, one's behavior pattern, people have assumed that "that's the way he is," "he can never change," it's to say he's less than a human being, which is the worst thing you can say about anybody; it's these rationalizations, defense mechanisms, excuses, not facing honestly that does finally numb, desensitize one's sense of self-criticism.

There's another reason it's a bad method: It does not get rid of the guilt at all. It simply puts blankets on top of it, and it sinks right down into the unconscious mind where it remains and festers and makes us ill in body as well as in soul. It is never, never digested. If enough accumulates, you have to open up with the aid of an expert—a psychiatrist or psychoanalyst. But it is never digested.

What is the way to reconcile honest self-criticism and healthy self-acceptance? What is the way to handle one's guilt? What can you do with it? Some years ago, in moving into a new summer place in Cape Cod, we got there late one night after driving up from New York, and had little time to pick up the things we needed. I did stop, however, along the way and got a few items to last through the first morning. Along with the food, I picked up one of those tri-cornered things you put in the corner of the sink. By 10 o'clock that was full, but I was going in again to stock up at a larger store. I picked up one of those cans you open with your foot. By the next day, that was full. My wife said: "Jim, we've got to face things more basically." So I went up to Provincetown in the station wagon and bought a great big galvanized can; in fact, I bought two of them. I brought them back and that was fine. Everything was great for a week. Finally she said: "What are we going to do?" Well, one thought occurred to me. You know in these new houses there is always a lot of closet space. We could have put our garbage in there. But, that wouldn't have been the healthy thing to do, would it? And it just isn't healthy to keep surpressing your sense of guilt by all of those excuses. I know you're wondering what we did up there at Cape Cod. We decided that we needed to have an outside agency take it off our hands.

This is the Christian answer to the problem. We believe in a God who has the resources to take all the guilt, the hurt, yes, the filth of the world into himself. That is what it means to be a Christian. That is what this is all about. We believe in a God who can take all this into himself and take it off us and free us and enable us to accept ourselves again.

This is the heart of the Christian faith. Man's central problem is in this realm and the heart of the gospel is the answer. That is why I became a Christian again after years of agnosticism when I was a lawyer. (By the way, you don't have to be an unbeliever to be a lawyer, but it helps.) But when I found that my central problem was met by what is the very center of the Christian faith, I knew that there must be sense to that faith. What this answer says is that I can *honestly* look at myself and turn it all over to him and he takes it away. "O Lamb of God that takest away the sins of the world." I can accept myself because he accepts me though I am unacceptable. This keeps the honesty in it and I don't need any excuses, defense mechanisms, rationalizations; I don't need to push the guilt down into my own unconscious mind. He takes up the slack between himself and me, and he meets me where I am and not where I ought to be. He fills the gap between the "ought" and the "is."

This gap I cannot fill. Why? Because the claim is total. I'm expected to give 100 per cent performance all the time. If I do something nice tomorrow, it doesn't make up for the wrong I did today, because I'm supposed to be nice tomorrow. I'm supposed to use all my time and talents in human relationship in the right way. I can't be more than perfect, and we're called upon to be perfect. Hence we can never make it up; we can never fill the gap. He fills the gap. Theologically speaking, this is called "justification by grace through faith."

What does that mean? "Justification" doesn't mean being right; it means being taken for right. It means being accepted. "By grace" means: I don't earn it; it's free. "Through faith" means believing the promise, having turned myself over and admitted that I'm in need. "Just as I am, without one plea," "in my hand no price I bring."

Justification by grace through faith, but that's not the end of the story. That would seem like quite a "free ride," for that reason this belief has "put off" people. To them it seems almost indecent that God should act in such a way. How does he keep his standards; how could he be a good God if he can accept me? That is a good question. The answer is: He does keep his standards, yet he does accept me. How does that happen? It's a mystery and we call it the Atonement. There are six or seven theories which Christians have thought up as to how that works, and no one of them is final or infallible. They're all suggestive. We never will know the mystery of the heart of God. In the book of Job we read, "Touching the Almighty, we cannot find him out." We'll never quite know. But in the Cross of Christ, he tipped his hand. There is a clue to all this in human relations when there is the breaking down of the wall of separation between two people. Somebody's got to take the heart; somebody's got to supply the grace. Someone's got to accept or there is no reconciliation. Even in human relations the text applies: "Without shedding of blood [there] is no remission of sins." So God keeps his standards, asserts his righteousness, and cares what we do. He doesn't say, "skip it." He gives us the dignity of his caring. And yet, he takes the hurt.

That is what the Cross everlastingly tells us. That is the image of God's doings on the scene of history. He does that. He always has and always will because that is the kind of God he is. Yet, what about us? Isn't it wrong that it is just this way and we do nothing? We, too, do something. True, we cannot be saved by our good works; we're saved by grace. But good works come into this scheme because for this precious gift, you are grateful, and gratitude provides a new motivation, a new dynamic for goodness. In thanksgiving, you want to be more acceptable. You want to become the way God has accepted you as being. You know how that is in personnel relationships. Some employee hasn't been doing too well and you reassure him, saying, "You're all right, you can do it, you've really got the know-how. You've really got the stuff." In gratitude for that the employee wants to be like you have accepted him as being. Often a child will react that way to his parents' acceptance. So it is here; you want to respond by being that which you have been accepted as being.

Paul explains "justification by grace through works" in Ephesians. You're not saved by works, but they are the fruit of having been saved by God's free grace.

What are we to be like as Christians in the world? Keep a lot of rules? Yes, that's helpful and some of our churches will vary as to the rules. But basically the Christian's response is deeper.

God accepts me though I'm unacceptable; as I'm supposed to accept other persons though I think they're unacceptable. God takes up the slack between himself and me, and I'm supposed to take up the slack between myself and others. God takes the hurt out of my life, and I'm supposed to be, as a Christian, an expert in taking hurt out of other people's life. Why? We're repeating the act. We're called to be coredeemers with Christ in this way, as we thankfully respond to his gift of redemption.

It is all summed up by one witness in that little epistle (by an unknown author) known as First John. It summarizes the theology and the ethics in one verse: "If God so loved us, we ought also to love one another." That is the whole thing. Justification by faith, through grace, unto good works. Or to put it in modern psychological terms, the reconciliation of self-criticism and self-acceptance. How do you practice this?

Don't let your guilt surround you at night as you're trying to go to sleep, thinking of this event and that conversation: the paper work unfinished on the desk—when people were counting on answers—not having given enough credit to someone or having claimed too much yourself, or some worse sins. I'm not mentioning the more obvious sins; you know about them. I'm talking about personal relations where we often fail in love and in duty. Don't start that record playing of excuses—that doesn't get rid of the guilt, doesn't help you change. Get the jump on these guilt feelings.

In some traditions, including my own, there is what is known as "examination of conscience." I don't know how often you dump your garbage at home but dump your guilt just as often. If you don't clean up your kitchen more than once a week at home, maybe you won't want to clean up your moral life more than once a week; but if you're on a daily basis for one clean-up, I think once a day is good for the other. Get it out of the house. Don't lock it in the closets. Don't leave it around or you'll feel bad about things. You won't be able to accept the situation and accept yourself. No, dump it. Here is what you do. Don't dump it before you make the most of it. Look over your day. Think of the people you met; were they better off or worse off for being with you? Think of what you did and didn't do. Think of what you could fix up and make mental notes of what you're going to do tomorrow: You're going to try to call someone; you're going to get that letter off or do what you're supposed to do. Things that you can't fix up, all right, that's that. Learn from it for the future. Then wrap it all up in a package. Ask God to take this and work on it, say something like this: "You've got all night, you're not sleeping anyway. Please take this away. I'm going to go to sleep. I'm going to try to feel fresh tomorrow, because—I'm so thankful for your taking all this away—I'm going to be more like you've taken me to be. Good night." This is the way to handle it. Now that prayer isn't in the *Book of Common Prayer* but it works well. For to carry all this around with you is just like having to pull a great big trailer full of junk attached to the car, and trying to maneuver in Washington traffic, trying to get up and down hills—all very clumsy. It bogs life down. Cut that rope, let the trailer go down the hill, and drive up in high gear. You're free; this is what we're meant to be in Jesus Christ.

For this precious gift which is in the heart of our faith, we should be eternally grateful. This is not only sound psychology and sound psychosomatic medicine; it is the gospel.

The Peace of God

JAMES I. MCCORD

☆☆☆ In the fourth chapter of Philippians, the seventh verse, are these words: "And the peace of God, which passeth all understanding, shall keep your hearts and minds through Christ Jesus."

Ralph Tyler Flewelling tells the story of how Dante, the great poet of the Middle Ages, when exiled from his home in Florence and cast down by the cruel turn of fate, determined to walk from Italy to Paris where he could study philosophy in an effort to find a clue to the riddle of man and his destiny. In his travels he found himself a weary pilgrim, forced to knock at the door of Santa Croce Monastery to find refuge from the night. A surly brother within was finally aroused, came to the door, flung it open, and in a gruff voice asked, "What do you want?" Dante answered in a single word, "Peace." And in this answer he expressed not only his deepest longing but the deepest aspiration of mankind.

But how is peace achieved? What is its source? From whence does it come? And even when we experience peace for a moment, how do we grasp it and keep it? All of the great religions and philosophies have wrestled with these questions. This was the case in China, where Confucius taught that peace comes to the man who lives a life of moderation, who indulges in nothing too much, and who manages to build up a life of perfect harmony and balance. It is the same question in India, but there the answer to peace is in terms of withdrawal from the world and all of its responsibilities, in order that man may be alone with the Alone. The ancient Stoics taught that peace comes from following nature, when one rises above the level of pain and pleasure and accepts things as they are.

In all of these instances peace is an achievement of man. It is something he must acquire for himself. It is a balance he builds up and then is forced to maintain. But when one looks at the New Testament, there is a different kind of peace altogether. "The peace of God," about which Paul writes, is a gift to be received not a balance to be achieved. It is not so much within man as without him. It is God's gift that comes down from above to surround man and to provide the context for his whole existence.

Paul had experienced this peace of God, and his problem was to explain it to the apostolic community at Philippi. You can almost see his mind work as he searches for the right words, when suddenly he hits upon a military figure of speech to express his meaning. He remembers that Philippi is a Roman colony, a boon conferred on the city by Caesar Augustus because it was here that he won his first great victory. As a Roman colony it had the protection of Roman legionnaires stationed in the city, whose job it was to keep the peace. Every Philippian could go to sleep at evening in full confidence that a guard had been posted and watch was being kept against the threat of any marauding Thracian from the north. Now it is precisely this figure—of a guard being posted and a watch being kept—that Paul uses to describe the peace of God in Christ Jesus.

Let us look at the components of the peace of God. First of all, it surely means that there is peace with God. We talk about our relation to God glibly, when we discuss it at all, and assume that religion as usual goes on at a steady pace. But when we are honest about our religious life, there is another story to tell. Things do not always run smoothly, do they? We have our ups and downs, our seasons of spiritual dryness, our personal deserts. We can understand Paul dying daily, Rachel weeping for her children, Job cursing his day, and the psalmist crying out, "My God, my God, why hast thou forsaken me?"

So universal is this experience of alienation that Alfred North White-head, the philosopher of the last generation, has claimed that man's relation to God generally follows the pattern of a rhythm in three beats. In the beginning the word "God" stands for nothing; there is nothing in man's experience to match it. Then as he grows older and his burden of guilt accumulates, God begins to stand for the enemy, the avenger. Only later, and often after deep suffering, does man come to understand that God is neither the void nor the enemy but the one who has come alongside him in Jesus Christ to accept him and to give him the possibility of a new life.

This knowledge of God did not come in the scriptures of the Old Testament until the experience of Hosea. He was a contemporary of the prophet, Amos, but Amos belonged to another people and was called to prophesy against Israel, Hosea's people. Amos seemed to glow with the righteous indignation of youth as he spoke of the God of the plumb line, who would execute his judgment on Israel. But Hosea, perhaps standing on the edge of the crowd as he listened to the fiery words of Amos, could see that God was indeed the God of judgment but also something more. Out of his own experience with a faithless woman whom he still loved he could see that there is nothing in God that wants to kick human life to bits, nothing that enjoys inflicting human suffering. There is only infinite love and mercy and compassion.

A generation ago the name of Dwight L. Moody could electrify two continents, so successful was he as an evangelist, but it was not always so. He had begun a business career in Chicago, only to leave it for work in a mission in the slums. But his ministry there lacked something, the people would drift away after a few weeks or months, and he seriously considered throwing in the towel and giving up the whole project as a bad job. At this point his wife, sensing his despair, convinced him that he should take a holiday abroad. While he was in Great Britain, he heard a series of sermons on the golden text of the Bible, John 3:16. "God so loved the world, that he gave his only begotten Son, that whosoever believeth in him should not perish, but have everlasting life." ("World" is for John a technical term. It means rebellious mankind organized in its

46

opposition against God.) As Moody heard this text expounded, he suddenly realized that his approach had been all wrong. He had been speaking of God as the one who follows man, stalking and threatening him, ready at any moment to reach out and cut him down in judgment. Now he learned that the heart of God is to be seen in the face of Jesus Christ. Wrath is not God's final word. Rather God's last word is Jesus Christ, Immanuel, God-with-us. It is God who comes to us in Christ, the God of peace, and he removes every obstacle that separates us from himself. We are not juggled about by blind and secondary forces, for One has come and has established our peace.

Consider, again, that the peace of God brings us peace with ourselves. Goethe had Faust cry out, "Two souls, alas, are lodged within my breast!" And we know that experience too. We know what it is to feel the tug and sway of giant forces that vie for dominion, and often we feel that their battleground is within our own souls. We know what it is to be pushed about to and fro, willy-nilly, by almost every current and crosscurrent that blows. We expend our energies, and we exhaust ourselves. We have made the mental institution and the psychiatrist the twin symbols of our culture. And what is there left but to cry with Paul, "O wretched man that I am! who shall deliver me?"

It was the late Ernest Fremont Tittle who asked, "What is man's greatest need?" He then answered his own question bluntly, "A master." Not something to serve us! We have had enough of this, for we have turned everything that we know to our own service. What we need is someone great enough and grand enough to command us, organize us, and give us a sense of direction and purpose. This is the meaning of peace with ourselves.

I am not speaking of a peace that will take away all of our tensions, for tension is the source of creativity. The gospel is no cheap trick to relieve us of responsibility for advance and progress. It is service to him who embodies the purpose of the living God and who calls us into the service of that purpose. Until we know this peace with ourselves, we are a divided people, unable to launch forth venturesomely on any course.

Finally, the peace of God brings us peace with others. It establishes us in a new context of relations and lifts us out of the egotism and prejudice that threaten the future of all mankind. Until we know this new dimension of peace, we constitute a part of the world's problem rather than part of its answer.

The problem is put better in a song from *South Pacific* than I could ever put it. Do you remember these words:

> You've got to be taught to hate and fear.
> You've got to be taught from year to year.
> It's got to be dinned in your dear little ear.
> You've got to be carefully taught.
>
> You've got to be taught to be afraid
> Of people whose eyes are oddly made,
> And people whose skin is a different shade.
> You've got to be carefully taught.
>
> You've got to be taught before it's too late,
> Before you're six or seven or eight,
> To hate all the folks your relatives hate.
> You've got to be carefully taught.[1]

And we have been carefully taught and we carefully teach. Hence we are a part of an unbroken chain of poisoned relations that threaten the fairest hopes of man.

The central affirmation of the New Testament is that this chain has been broken by him who refused to become a link in the chain of poisoned relations and who took man's prejudice and hatred upon himself in order that they might end there.

A few years ago I saw this interpretation of Christ's work vividly illustrated in a wood carving in a church in Germany. Prior to World War II, a huge edifice had stood on this spot where God has been worshiped since the days of the Saxons, but in three days and nights of saturation bombing the church was obliterated. Even the trees in the churchyard were blown down. When the war ended, the people came creeping out of their warrens and hovels and began immediately to rebuild a house of worship. They could afford only a bare rectangular structure, and then they added wood carvings by an eccentric genius from the Rhine-

---

[1] "You've Got to Be Carefully Taught." Copyright © 1949 by Richard Rodgers and Oscar Hammerstein II. Williamson Music, Inc., New York, N. Y., owner of publication and allied rights.

land. He used the wood of the trees that had been blown down, and carved twelve apostles and a heroic statue of Christ. It is that Christ, with his imperfections, that rivets one's attention. Shrapnel protrudes from the shoulder, steel is visible in his side, and his kneecap is broken. The woodcarver had made no attempt to remove the bits of the bomb that had lodged in the wood of the tree. What was he saying? What man had used for murder and destruction, Christ has taken into himself, and never again will it be used for this purpose. This is what he can do for us, with our prejudices and our fears. He can lift us into a new level of personal relations where there is peace and understanding.

We are moving toward the climax of the Lenten season. All of the great events of the drama of redemption will unfold before us—the triumphal entry, Good Friday, and the glorious Easter morn—with the affirmation of victory over death. My Lenten prayer for you is that you may know the peace of God, which transcends our understanding, but which, like a Roman legionnaire posted as a watch, guards you through Christ Jesus.

Stand Fast in Liberty

HENRY I. LOUTTIT

☆☆☆ Part of the first verse of the fifth chapter of the Epistle of Paul the Apostle to the Galatians is quoted: "Stand fast therefore in the liberty wherewith Christ hath made us free." These words of Paul must come as a crucial call to every Christian in these days of tension, struggle, and warfare. Once again our adversary, the devil, walketh about as a roaring lion seeking whom he may devour, this time under the guise of an atheistic, materialistic communism. The all-out struggle in the world between Russia, China, and their subject satellites and the United States, the free world, and her allies is a complex affair embracing political, national, economic, ideological and philosophical aspects. Still it will never truly be understood until we realize that ultimately it is a clash between two universal religions, each offering salvation to every man, and hence each demanding the loyalty of every man.

My first point is simply that we will never understand communism until we see it as it is, a Judeo-Christian heresy, a twisted and distorted offshoot of our common Judeo-Christian religious heritage. This is evidenced by its structure; whether conscious or unconscious, I know not.

It claims, as we all know, to be atheistic, but it has a supreme power historical necessity, or speaking more precisely, dialectic materialism. It, too, has a messiah in one Karl Marx. It has a sacred scripture in *Das Kapital* and the Communist Manifesto. It, too, has a Peter and Paul in Lenin and Khrushchev with the politburo as the college of the apostles.

It, too, has a chosen people—in theory, of course—the proletariat or the workers of the world; in actual fact, from Moscow's point of view, the Russians; from the point of view of Peiping, the Chinese people, which gives a ray of hope. It has a worldwide evangelistic and missionary program which puts in the shade the pathetically inadequate effort of the Christian church to win the world. Above all, it has a messianic vision, an apocalyptic vision of a new and better social order. A perfect social order brought about not by the coming of a messiah or the second coming of our Lord to inaugurate his kingdom and his eternal reign, but brought about by the catastrophic intervention of a worldwide workers' revolution.

Now, quite obviously, this universal religion which claims and wins the absolute commitment and utter devotion of men without thought of cost or sacrifice clashes with, and only with, the Christian faith which dares to make the same demand for absolute and utter commitment to our Lord and Saviour, Jesus Christ, the incarnate Son of God.

My second point is simply this. You and I must recognize the fact that our freedom, our democracy, our way of life rests on one foundation only, the Christian faith. It is based on the Christian premise that man is made in the image of God and, therefore, has certain inalienable rights and dignities. This is seen in history where freedom and democracy, the right of every man to have a voice in government, is known and only known where the Christian gospel has been preached and, in part at least, received. This truth is further underlined by the fact that every dictator, whether Nazi or Communist, avows enmity to the death of the Christian church. This we should know.

In the history of the founding of our nation, our life began with a people who left home and kindred, the ways of comfort and security, to traverse an unknown sea to pioneer in a bitter and hostile wilderness for one reason and only one reason, that they might worship God in accordance with the dictates of their own conscience.

The first English-speaking settlers landed in Virginia and began our corporate life with a celebration of the Holy Communion in accordance with the *Book of Common Prayer*. The next settlers who landed in New England, the Pilgrim fathers, began their corporate existence by signing the Mayflower Compact, the first written democratic constitution in the history of mankind which opened, "In the Name of God." By and large, the early colonists accepted the philosophy of William Penn, "Men must be governed by God or they will be ruled by tyrants." This is why, at the beginning of our history, we could adopt as a motto, "In God We Trust."

Since our founding fathers accepted the Christian philosophy of history as revealed in Scripture, they could preface the charter of our liberties, the Declaration of Independence, with the firmest affirmation of Christian faith that the English language is capable of expressing. It acknowledges the self-evident truths of God's existence and his supreme place as Creator and Father of mankind. It extolls the brotherhood of man on the basis of a God-given equality of all men. It even defines government as an agency to secure the God-given rights of men.

The choice lies clear, we may accept willingly or unwillingly the final degradation of slavery under an atheistic, Communistic dictatorship or we must commit ourselves anew to Christ and his church, which is to consecrate ourselves to the demanding tasks of ensuring freedom and democracy for the world of men, that peace may reign.

In 1959, Max Ways wrote a brilliant study entitled *Beyond Survival*, which gives much food for thought. His thesis is very simple, Men need a greater vision than merely to survive. Thus far we seem to be on the defensive only.

American life, indeed, life in the Western world, needs meaning, needs purpose, needs a goal as it is engaged in this all-out struggle with communism which has dedicated itself to the domination of the world by atheistic materialism. Once again we must embrace the philosophy of our founding fathers, who in signing the Declaration of Independence, pledged their lives, their fortunes, and their sacred honor to the new kind of nation which was struggling to be born. To us, as to them, there must be something higher than mere survival. They pledged their lives. To us, as to them, there must be something higher than mere personal or national interest. They pledged their fortunes. There must be something as demanding as the laws of nature and of nature's God—the moral restraint, the higher responsibility, the greater vision of freedom and justice and democracy for the world of men under the divine imperative that God made man in his own image and, consequently, he has certain inalienable rights and dignities. They pledged their sacred honor. We live or die as a society, we succeed or fail as we go forward with the idea of order, the idea of freedom, and the idea of God intertwined, or as sleep-walkers with the instruments of destruction in our hands.

For a churchman the call comes clear. We must dictate ourselves to that better social order which we call God's kingdom where his rule reigns. Of this, the church, your church, is at once the pledge, the earnest, and God's instrument and agency for its accomplishment. That Christ may reign now is the program of the church. That we may reign with him eternally is the Christian promise of salvation.

As a nation, as a moral nation, certainly we must remain on the defensive only in regard to the use of military force. But we must maintain that force in the first place, as a deterrent to all-out and bloody warfare which threatens total destruction through the use of missile and nuclear power; and in the second place, and quite as important, as an effectual symbol that to us, at least, freedom is of greater value than mere life.

But basically, this is a war of ideas, of ideals, of living faiths, and it can never be won on battlefields, but necessitates winning the hearts, the minds, the wills, the loyalties of men. This then is the task and program of the church. Christ must reign in the heart of every man, in all society, and over all creation. His rule must be supreme in every personal and social relationship: military, national, political, economic, commercial, international, social, racial. If Christ is King of necessity there needs to be a social order, a Kingdom, over which he reigns. But in the long last, a better society can only be built of better men, a perfect society only out of perfected, sanctified men.

For two thousand years the church has accepted just this challenge and has labored unceasingly that men might be converted and perfected and sanctified. The measure of her success is witnessed by the vast host of men, sung and unsung, known and unknown, who were changed from craven cowards to faithful heroes, not counting the cost, embracing martyrdom, to serve their King. Through twenty centuries by word, by worship, by sacrament, she has transformed sinners, repentant and forgiven, into saints, soldiers of the eternal Lord. This is the choice—Christ or that chaos out of which communism may emerge supreme. This is the challenge: that you and I commit ourselves, all that we are, all that we have, all that we do, to him, to his way of life, which is the way of love, the way of sacrifice, the way of the Cross, but the way of salvation for every man. This is the hope, the only hope, that thereby God in Christ may yet save this doomed, damned, and hence desperate world. "Stand fast therefore in the liberty wherewith Christ hath made us free."

New Wineskins

ELTON TRUEBLOOD

☆ ☆ ☆ Whenever we have any temptation to complacency in our religious life, the words of Jesus Christ are always an antidote to that complacency. The fiercest enemies of Christ were not the pagans. The fiercest enemies of Christ were always those who were religious people. Apparently it was with them in mind that he produced the parable of the new wine and the new skins. He said, "No one puts new wine into old wineskins; if he does, the new wine will burst the skins and it will be spilled, and the skins will be destroyed. But new wine must be put into new wineskins." (Luke 5:37-38 RSV.)

The importance of this parable is seen in the fact that it appears in three of the Synoptic Gospels, in Matthew, in Mark, and in Luke. And in each it appears in the same context. What he is saying is that the spiritual life, to be real, must always be fresh and new. The skins get older and, when they do, we have nothing because the fermenting of new wine brings pressure upon the old skins and they crack at their seams. Thus everything will be lost. What Christ says, then, is that we must continually find new, fresh, and vivid ways in which to reach the spiritual life of men and women. To put it in another way, he is saying that the one thing that you cannot do in this world is to maintain a plateau. If you are not advancing, you are already decaying. If we are not going forward, we are going backward. In the nature of the world we cannot maintain permanently a fixed position. Therefore we must in our religious life always be breaking the stereotypes. Our task is to crack them, and to crack them by the explosive growing power of the new fermenting wine of the Spirit.

This is a time of tremendous novelty so far as the spiritual life of man is concerned. For example: There is a Christian coffee house on Columbia Road here in Washington. It has no ecclesiastical symbols. It does not exist in order to support any church. It does not exist to make money or to support any organization. It is simply a place for people, including those who are uprooted and lonely, to come together and to be given a chance, under the care of sincere Christians, to have an evening of the confrontation of ideas. Some may receive answers to their questions, if questions they have. Following this successful beginning in Washington, D.C., other such places are being started at many points across our land.

Another example is that provided by the lay academies. There was a day when we had, of course, the theological seminaries for men who wanted to become pastors or chaplains of the armed forces or to be professional clergymen. We still have excellent seminaries of this character, as we should have, but now the new thing is the developing of lay academies. These are institutions where men and women who are in common life, who are in business, who are not professional can take a little time out of their everyday happenings and can study what it means to be good servants to Jesus Christ right on the firing-line of their ordinary duties. A new one has opened in Texas, for example, where forty people can come together at a time and where enormous changes come in their lives. Often they grow more in forty-four hours there than they do in forty-four weeks in ordinary life at home.

Another new development is what we call vocational evangelism. We see that men and women care a great deal about their daily work. Doctors care about being good doctors. Singers care about being good singers. Lawyers care about being good lawyers. So one of the freshest things in the contemporary religious life is the organization of men and women along their line of vocation.

For example: One great American city has had a group of doctors spending an entire year on the oath of Hippocrates. Bishop Pike, having himself been a lawyer before he became a clergyman, has done much to let us see what a ministry the law may become. It is easy to see that this has untold possibilities as men and women employ imagination to learn how to apply this idea to a variety of occupations.

I have had the opportunity of doing this for military men of America now stationed in France, Germany, and Italy. One of the most exciting things that I know is the way that the military men are raising funds in order to endow a scholarship and to establish a chair of theology in Japan. They are doing it as men of the armed forces, as an expression of their ministry and their new lives in Christ. Here I have given just a few examples of the way in which this fresh life is appearing. I need not take time to give you more, but I want you to know that these are only the barest beginnings of what is possible.

In churches we find new life. Today there are prayer groups meeting in factories, in offices, and in clubs across the length and breadth of our land. The time is past when it was sufficient to think that we could meet the needs of the day with three hymns and a sermon and a benediction. These may be good, but they are not good enough. They are the old wineskins and Christ has told us that our task is to find new ones.

The most thrilling thing that I know about our faith is this: *It is continually new.* We are living in one of the early days of the faith. Ten thousand years from now your descendants and mine, if there are any descendants, and if the faith that we affirm today is still alive, will look back upon this time and they will say: "They were in the early days. They were in the days when the faith was still growing. They were the days when the faith of Jesus Christ still, like new wine, was fermenting and growing and cracking the old forms because of its inner vitality."

I believe this is true. We are alive in the days when the faith is still in ferment.

The Cross and the Way Life Is

ROBERT B. MCNEILL

☆ ☆ ☆ "My kingdom does not belong to this world" (NEB), said Jesus to Pilate in that memorable dialogue on the subject of authority and truth. I am no competitor of yours, I will not contest you here, you can be sovereign in your kind of world. I am not and never will be lord of the way things are, I am not chief of a kingdom of compromise and weak concession. No, Pilate, said Jesus, I am regent of another kind of world which I am pitting against yours, your world of the way life is.

The way life is? What shall we say about it? It is predatory. One order of life lives upon another. Alexander King said that there is a civil war going on beneath the sod of every well-trimmed lawn. The lower forms of insect life struggle against one another for survival and above hops an innocent looking robin ready to capture the first unsuspecting worm that comes to the surface. When our yellow tomcat slinks off into the woods nearby, the chipmunks had better scurry to their caves and the field mice to their holes. In the meantime the cat must avoid the neighbor's boxer or he might never return from his prowl. The hound stalks the fox, the fox the otter, the otter the trout, the trout the fly. The weaker the species the more numerous it is, both to provide food for others and preserve itself. Nature doesn't favor particular creatures, only their classifications.

Above them all stands man, capable of preying upon all the others, and he does so, if not for food for fun. But man distinguishes his breed by preying on his own kind. Once he stuffed his belly with his slain enemy, consuming (he thought) his courage as well as his flesh. Now in his sophistication he desires neither the flesh nor the courage of another; he is content with his subjugation and his labor. He achieves this by what he cynically calls the law of the jungle. He has gone the beasts one better—even the lions would fear to prowl his kind of jungle.

From the beginning of civilization some muscular tribe has ravaged the earth as far as it could go. Egypt, Assyria, Persia, Greece, Rome (and here stood Pilate as representative of time's most relentless and successful predator), the barbaric tribes of Europe, France, Germany, Turkey, Mongolia, Britain. We have called it exploitation, colonialism, conquest, and even liberation, but the dark factor in it all is that man is still willing to steal from and kill his own kind. And what will history record about Russia—and about us? What monstrous specter is man when he preys upon his own. That's the way life is, we shrug. But Christ does not preside over this.

The way life is? It is competitive. We rather like that word—the key word, we say, to the American way of life. It makes us think of a hustling young insurance salesman making the million dollar round table or red-blooded giants knocking heads in a football stadium for the glory of the college or brilliant young scientists developing new fabrics or plastics to win back the foreign market. So we press it upon all areas of life. If father consents to manage a little league team, his boys must win the pennant even at the expense of the game's enjoyment. If teenage daughter is pretty, she must prove it by winning beauty pageants. If young son is brilliant, he must prove his genius by winning monetary awards dangled before him by foundations and by industry. It is not enough to improve and to achieve, we must beat somebody at something.

> Saul has slain his thousands,
> And David his ten thousands. (RSV.)

We compete especially in the accumulation of money. As in all competition there are more losers than winners. On a national scale the consistent losers clamor to rearrange our economy, and on the international they become the have-not nations. Winners are seldom secure. They do take anxious thought for what they eat and drink and put on, no matter how luxurious and abundant. Anxiety to get is exceeded by anxiety to keep. That's the way life is. But Christ does not preside over this.

The way life is? It is stratified. We have rejoiced that old systems of caste and class are disappearing. Unfortunately, new ones take their places. Once we were born into one and were taught to accept and enjoy it whether high or low. Now we struggle into a stratum of society and struggle to stay there, never secure. The symbols of that status may be skin color, a barbecue grill, military chevrons, or church affiliation. Why do we wish to be stratified? Maybe it's because there is a bit of the snob in each of us, and if we must mix with people we want the company of those who will adorn us and who will never be an object of real concern. Why not "water seeks its own level" and "birds of a feather" and all that? That's the way life is. But Christ does not preside over this.

The way life is? It is painful. But here man takes a positive stance. He is willing for life to be predatory, competitive, stratified but not painful. There is no way to use pain to his advantage and it plays no favorites so he is out to eradicate it. And until he does it is to be avoided at all costs, even at the cost of his honesty and integrity. He should not be required to suffer, so yield the point, strike the colors, suspend convictions rather than endure any form of it whether it be physical hurt, mental anguish, or common anxiety. Indeed life is painful and we must practice the escape of it for that's the way life is. But Christ does not preside over this.

The way life is? It is fatal. Death stalks us from birth. We are always just a disease away from it. It leers at us on the highways. It grins expectantly at the wrinkling skin, the dimming eye, and laboring breath. "Neither kings nor princes one moment can retard the appointed hour." When we are finally willing to concede our mortality, death may loom as the one stark fact that no one can challenge, perhaps the only believable fact to some who see no meaning to life once they have admitted it. So devoid of significance life is a brief candle and an idiot's tale. That's the way life is. But Christ does not preside over this.

If that's the way life is, there are two questions to be asked. The first is, why did God make it this way? I am not so sure that he did. Maybe this is our paradise lost. We certainly perpetuate this life as though we preferred it and originated it. The second question is, why doesn't God do something to change it? The answer to that is that he has. He has not changed human nature by performing a lobotomy while under anesthetic. This would deprive man of his right to choose and to care. No, God confronted man in person, in the person of Christ. More than that, he put the whole realm of life as it was, in tension with his own regency. "I have not come to bring peace [on the earth], but a sword" (RSV), said Christ. Not the peace of compromise with the way life is but a sword which radically cleaves a man from an unredemptive environment and unredeeming associations (even the members of one's own family). Only by this tension created by Christ could man finally realize that his daily struggle was against God; only by this tension and man's ultimate exhaustion from it could there be reconciliation and redemption.

Let's see how this tension was created. Life is predatory we say? Whom we exploit we will first call an enemy. But how contrary this is to Christ's way for he said, "Love your enemies, bless them that curse you, do good to them that hate you, and pray for [not prey upon] them which despitefully use you."

Life is competitive? Jesus himself was probably a better craftsman than the neighboring carpenters but he did not make a religion of winning. In fact, his sympathies lay with the losers. Blessed are you poor, he said— while he had some pretty sobering words for the big winners—"But alas for you who are rich; you have had your time of happiness" (NEB).

Life is stratified? Here is an up-ending of our caste system—"Let the greatest among you become as the youngest, and the leader as one who serves" (RSV).

Life is painful? Yes it is, but suffering itself is not an evil and it must be borne if one's integrity is at stake. Dietrich Bonhoeffer points out that suffering may be our witness and our communion with God. Jesus said:

Be on your guard, for men will hand you over to their courts, they will flog you in the synagogues, and you will be brought before governors and kings, for my sake, to testify before them and the heathen. [There is our witness.] But when you are arrested, do not worry about what you are going to say; . . . for it is not you who will be speaking: it will be the Spirit of your Father speaking in you. [And there is our communion.] (NEB.)

Life is fatal? It is if the world is too much for us, if mortal flesh is our only trust. But this radical Christ dared claim, "I am the resurrection and the life: he that believeth in me, though he were dead, yet shall he live." Life then will be as fatal or as fullsome as we make it.

Christ brought this tension upon man and man's action was to crucify him and be at peace. But peace he had not had. And peace he will not have until he ceases to crucify on one hand and on the other to rely upon some cultic spattering of blood for his redemption. Blood was shed, yes, but not by divine ritual; it was by man's life and death struggle against God.

A choice is upon us here, between the way life is and the way Christ lives. We have not been honest, we have wanted to take a little of both but this choice is not open to us. This doesn't mean that we must withdraw from one world to live in another. It means that we must, as agents of Christ, impose one upon the other until convention becomes conversion. It is written, "A disciple is not above his teacher . . . it is enough for the disciple that he be as his master." And in what way are we to be like him? "If any man will come after me, let him deny himself, and take up his cross, and follow me. For whosoever will save his life shall lose it: and whosoever will lose his life for my sake [and the gospel's] shall find it."

The Lamb of God

ROBERT P. TAYLOR

☆☆☆ Two thousand years ago Jesus was described by John the Baptist as, "the Lamb of God."

How does this appellation of Jesus as the Lamb of God relate to what he accomplished by his death on the cross? There is a sense in which John the Baptist summed up both the heart and the whole of the Christian gospel in the phrase, "the Lamb of God."

To you and me the word "lamb" suggests gentleness, meekness, and humility. It connotes patience, purity, innocence. Now, of course, Jesus embodied these qualities. To John's hearers, however, the idea of "lamb" suggested something very different.

A lamb, in the minds of the group to whom John spoke, signified sacrifice. The streams of ancient ritual and prophecy converged on this metaphor, and the image which emerged was a sacrificial offering. Their minds must have harkened back to the familiar prophecies: "The Lord hath laid on him the iniquity of us all. . . . He is brought as a lamb to the slaughter, and as a sheep before her shearers is dumb, so he openeth not his mouth. . . . By his knowledge shall my righteous servant justify many; for he shall bear their iniquities." John the Baptist looked back to these beloved prophecies, then pointed to Jesus of Nazareth standing by his side and said that here they are fulfilled. "Behold the Lamb of God, which taketh away the sins of the world."

What John is saying here is that Jesus Christ is the world's sinbearer. The sacrificial lamb, which was offered daily upon the altar, like the lamb slain at the Passover, symbolized deliverance from bondage. As the Lamb of God, Jesus Christ is the Saviour of the world.

Ancient prophecies, however, did not exhaust references to the sacrificial lamb for John's audience. They must have remembered the reference to the lamb in the story of a father and son trudging up Mount Moriah. Only the father knew what had to be done. He must sacrifice his son upon a lonely altar. The young Isaac, not knowing he was marked for slaughter, asked innocently, "Where is the lamb for a burnt offering?" Abraham replied, "My son, God will provide himself a lamb." John is implying in the phrase "the lamb of God" that here is the sacrifice on whom is laid the sins of the world. God himself had provided a lamb to save the world as nineteen centuries before he had provided a substitute offering and saved the lad Isaac.

It is significant to note here the connection between John's presentation of Jesus as the Saviour and the message of the angel who announced Jesus' birth. The angel did not say, "I bring you tidings of great joy for unto you is born this day in the city of David, a man, a good man, or a great man." He did not proclaim the coming of a religious genius, a teacher or a king. No, "Unto you is born this day in the city of David a Saviour, who is Christ the Lord." At the very beginning of his life on earth Jesus was heralded as a Saviour. Here again at the beginning of his ministry his friend, John the Baptist, reemphasized the purpose of Jesus' coming into the world. He was to save men from their sins. Today we look back to that cross on which he gave himself as the sacrificial Lamb of God.

The idea of Christ as Saviour of the world has two significant implications.

First, it implies that man is sinful. Now this is not a popular teaching. We do not like the idea of being evil. There are four witnesses who bear testimony, however, to the truth of this implication.

The Bible is forthright about man's condition. "All we like sheep have gone astray," says Isaiah, "we have turned every one to his own way." "All have sinned, and come short of the glory of God," says Paul. And the author of First John continues in the same vein, "If we say that we have no sin, we deceive ourselves, and the truth is not in us." That adds up to plain talk about the sinfulness of man.

Another witness is history. As one reads history there is little enough of sweetness and light. Man's inhumanity to man seems to have been the rule, not the exception, in human relationships. Greed, hate, injustice, deceit, blood, and tears have been the order of the day on many of history's pages. If I read history right, it is saying to us that there is something radically wrong with man which needs changing. To put it in religious terms—man is sinful.

Your own observation has something to say about the nature of man. Consider the evil acts you read about in the morning paper. Look at the potential and actual crisis abroad in the world today. Think of the tensions and the lack of goodwill that exist in what we think of as ordinary segments of our society. Our communities are shot through with people at sixes and sevens with themselves and with one another. Does not all this add weight to the proposition that man is sinful?

One last witness is called introspection. Let us take a look at our own hearts. An honest inward look is never flattering. Are we never indifferent to human needs? Are we never negligent in our opportunities to serve? "To him that knoweth to do good, and doeth it not, it is sin," says James. Who of us has not been circumscribed by that dictum? Or look at this matter of plain selfishness. Who of us can say that essentially and basically he is not selfish, self-seeking, and egocentric? As we look into our own hearts and see ourselves for what we are, who among us can say other than with the publican, "God, be merciful to me a sinner"?

These four bear a concerted testimony: Scripture, history, observation, and introspection agree—the evil that is within man is somehow deeply ingrained in the human race.

The second implication is a corollary of the first. It is that man needs a Saviour. Either sin is heinous in God's sight or it is of no consequence. If sin is a serious matter, then something or someone somehow must come onto the scene and do something about it.

John the Baptist had the answer. It was his conviction that Jesus Christ was the Lamb of God, the Saviour of the world. The death of Christ on the cross, was God's answer to the problem of man's evil. Christ took upon himself the sins of the world and became, for us, the Saviour.

Calvary was God's solution to what Billy Graham calls the "root cause" of man's problems. Man, both before and since, has tried in other ways to deal with evil within himself. The materialists—and one form of materialism is communism—have cut the Gordian knot by denying the fact of man's sinfulness.

They would admit, however, that man needs to be improved but this can be arranged by surrounding him with a proper environment, indoctrination, and education. There is nothing wrong with man, they say, that can't be cured by feeding him, clothing him, housing him, and educating him.

The Christian view of man is quite different. We say man needs a new start, a new birth, a new life. The familiar vocabulary for Christians in this connection includes repentance, atonement, reconciliation, and regeneration. At the heart of these great ideas is the theme that Jesus Christ came into the world not primarily to be our example nor to teach nor to befriend nor to lead but specifically to give us a change of heart. The writer to the Hebrews sums it up, "So Christ was once offered to bear the sins of many; and unto them that look for him shall he appear the second time without sin unto salvation."

The tragedy of the Cross is not the end of this story. It is the triumph of the Resurrection that gives meaning to all that goes before. Jesus Christ as the Lamb of God has significance only in light of victory over the grave.

Years ago, near the conclusion of World War II, I went up on the deck of a Japanese prison ship in the China Sea to conduct a burial service for an army colonel. As his body was lowered gently into the water it remained suspended a moment on the surface. A mighty wave then picked up the body, held it above the breast of the sea, and then deposited it into the salty deep. Above that wave was lifted sprays from the sea. Across that misty scene the sun shown and a perfect rainbow appeared. Those of us who looked upon that scene felt in our hearts that we had received a message from God. Here in the rainbow we saw God's promise and we were reminded vividly, "Death is swallowed up in victory. O death, where is thy sting? O grave, where is thy victory? . . . Thanks be to God, which giveth us the victory through our Lord Jesus Christ."

So today we use this symbol of "the Lamb of God" to call to our remembrance the meaning of Christ's death. Our Easter experience can be meaningful and can cause true rejoicing only as we lay hold of this significance of the Lamb's sacrificial death.

The Relevance of Calvary

JOSEPH R. SIZOO

☆☆☆ The heart of the world is kneeling once again before the most moving story that was ever written. The last hours in the life of our Lord are among the sublimest memories of earth. Betrayed by those he trusted, abandoned by those he loved, scourged by those he pitied, with a scarlet camp mantle flung contemptuously across his shoulders, crowned with a crown of thorns, he carried his cross to an outlaw's grave. Calvary seemed to the disciples an irretrievable disaster. Golgotha scarred their souls. It seemed the end of everything.

Yet such is the irony of history that more prayers are said by more people in more countries with their faces to that hill, on which stood a rugged cross, than any other spot on earth. Up and down this world, in every land and language, innumerable multitudes join with us in singing, "In the cross of Christ I glory." Carlyle called it "the water shed of history." Something happened there that has forever changed the history of the world. Perhaps you cannot understand it, but those who embrace it find that their hearts are strangely transformed.

This Cross stands central in the Christian tradition. You may conceive of Christianity without a ritual; you may conceive of Christianity without a church; you may conceive of Christianity without an organization, but to suppose you can think of Christianity without a Cross is as anomalous as it is impossible. We have embossed it on prayer books; we have emblazoned it on church spires; we have smothered it with roses, fulfilling the promise of him who said, "And I, if I be lifted up from the earth, will draw all men unto me."

The one symbol that has held Christendom together is the Cross. It is a sobering and tragic fact that what was meant to unite has so often divided, what was meant to draw men together has driven them apart. But somehow in the Cross all differences are forgotten. We have many systems of belief, but only one gospel. We have many ministers and priests, only one Saviour. We have many altars, only one Lamb of God. We have many creeds, only one Cross. So through the tumbling of the centuries, the fellowship of Jesus has recited and united in affirming, "I believe . . . in Jesus Christ . . . who . . . suffered under Pontius Pilate, was crucified, dead, and buried."

Why is that so significant? What is the relevance of Calvary to us in this year?

Calvary is the confrontation of two contrasting philosophies. At the Cross two ways of life that are mutually exclusive come into collision. The one philosophy relates man to the material and the tangible. The other philosophy relates man to the spiritual and the intangible. One measures life on the horizontal level, the other measures life on the vertical basis. And when the horizontal and the vertical clash, they always make a cross.

Take the first. Calvary is the meeting place of those who live life on the horizontal level, who concern themselves with material considerations. It was the voice of greed. Judas said, "How much will you give me?" He believed that everybody had his price. Every decision he made was based on the philosophy, "What can I get out of it?" So one day he betrayed his Master for thirty pieces of silver, $150. He put the dollar sign above the Cross.

It was the voice of religious intolerance. Caiaphas and the religious sybarites were the money changers at the Temple. They profited by vested interests. They were only concerned with outward conformity. They had no interest in inner loyalty to truth. Jesus interfered with their way of life, and they were determined to rid the world of him. It was either rule or ruin with them.

It was the voice of political compromise. Pilate said, "I find no fault in him." And in the next minute he surrenders him to be crucified. Pilate's only concern was the interest of the state. That was supreme. The individual was not much and did not matter. One Jew more or less meant nothing to him. The state must survive, and his position must prevail.

These were the three voices that sent our Lord to his cross: greed, religious intolerance, and political compromise. So they said of him, "Let him come down from the cross, and we will believe him." Come down to our level, do it our way, live by our philosophy, and we'll accept you.

Strangely enough these voices still prevail today. Calvary is not only an event in history but an ongoing tragedy of the world. The same three voices still speak. It is a rather significant and sobering fact that in the nineteenth century three men walked into history. They were Nietzsche, Freud, and Karl Marx. The first was a sick philosopher who signed his last letter, "The crucified one." The second was a miscalculating physician who traced all motivation back to sex and glands. The third was an improvident and hungry economist who believed that civilization and history were the inevitable product of the inexorable law of economic determinism. The first robbed modern man of his conscience. The second robbed modern man of his discipline. The third robbed modern man of his soul. Now in the twentieth century we are paying dearly for the voices of these three false messiahs.

They have created a society devoid of ends. It is a philosophy which maintains that a man is entitled to anything he can put his hands upon. Its creed is, "Get what you can; get it honestly if you can, but get it." They can eat caviar while a neighbor starves; they can play solitaire on Persian rugs while slum children stumble by because of malnutrition; they can pick flowers on Golgotha while the Son of God dies and leave him hanging in the rain. That philosophy sets class against class and sect against sect and race against race. It twists the lives of people out of shape and poisons the roots of being. It is nailing Christ to his cross once again. There have been more martyrs to Christ in the last forty years than in the first one thousand years of Christian history. That philosophy goes out with an exclamation point and a question mark blistered over with tears.

Over against the philosophy of the horizontal is the philosophy of the vertical. There stands the Son of God. He dragged the sorrows of his generation across his soul. He could not keep himself out of the welter and misery of men. He cared what happened to the reed that was bruised, to the lily that faded, to the sheep that was lost, and to the prodigal who stepped across the threshold of indiscretion. He healed another's scratch; his own side bled. Little children ran at the music of his voice. The sick were content to touch the hem of his garment, while the aged found comfort in his presence. He went out into that world saying, "My kingdom is not of this world." In the upper room of a widow's home in Jerusalem he met with his disciples, broke bread, and said, "Take, eat, this is my body which is broken for you." As if to say, you can drain my blood and break my bones, but you can't stop me from loving you.

Courage in war is common enough. But courage to face the defeat of goodwill and then pray forgiveness for those who have turned on you, that is true courage. That is Calvary. It means being true to yourself through the worst perversity that can be contrived against you.

That way of life is never easy. It sent Jesus to his cross. This is an insane world in which we live. We spend half of our time praying for saviours and the other half of the time nailing them to crosses. Ask Washington at Valley Forge or Lincoln at Ford's Theater or Joan of Arc on her way to her execution or Edith Cavell before the firing squad or the sailors on the Murmansk run or the marines at Iwo Jima or the soldiers on the Normandy beachhead or Albert Schweitzer in the long-grass jungle country of Africa—"What did you get out of it?" They would have said, "We got nothing out of it but tears and anguish and pain and struggle." But what a difference they have made. Carlyle was right, "Not what you possess but what you do with what you have determines your true worth."

It is a difficult way, but we know from history it can never, never be ultimately defeated. The Cross stands undimmed and unflickering on the broken skyline of the world, bringing hope and healing to all who are caught in the storm, the darkness, and the tensions of contemporary life.

I submit to you that I would be a cynic but for that one hour on

Calvary. Good Friday holds the essence of everything that makes the good worth struggling for. On Good Friday the world said no. On Easter God said yes. Issues in which Jesus Christ has a stake may be deferred and postponed, but they never can be ultimately defeated. Truth, justice, freedom, and love have in them the stuff of eternity. Pontius Pilate never speaks the last word. "He shall see the travail of his soul, and shall be satisfied."

We need people today who will come out boldly for the values for which Christ died, which they will not barter for gold no matter who snubs or who sneers or who screams. What Carlyle wrote at the close of the Napoleonic era is true of us, "The clock of the world might have been set forward a thousand years if there had been enough moral and religious forces to rebuild our shattered civilization upon a new and Christian foundation."

By which one of these two philosophies will you live? Sooner or later this world will have to make up its mind which it will be.

> To every man there openeth
> A Way, and Ways, and a Way.
> And the High Soul climbs the High Way,
> And the Low Soul gropes the Low,
> And in between, on the misty flats,
> The rest drift to and fro.
> But to every man there openeth
> A High Way, and a Low.
> And every man decideth
> The Way his soul shall go.[1]

Let us pray: God of the nations, God of our fathers, our God, if thou hast searched our hearts and found us wanting, forgive us for having lived with values unworthy of ourselves and thee. Help us as a people to recover these ideals and so become the highway for the Prince of Peace. For thy name's sake. Amen.

[1] "The Ways" from *Bees in Amber* by John Oxenham. Used by permission of Miss Theo Oxenham.

The Way of the Cross

J. FLOYD DREITH

> Go to dark Gethsemane,
>   Ye that feel the tempter's power;
> Your Redeemer's conflict see,
>   Watch with Him one bitter hour;
> Turn not from His griefs away,
>   Learn of Jesus Christ to pray!
>
> .   .   .   .   .   .
>
> Follow to the judgment hall,
>   View the Lord of Life arraigned;
> O the wormwood and the gall!
>   O the pangs His soul sustained!
> Shun not suffering, shame, or loss,—
>   Learn of Him to bear the Cross.[1]

★ ★ ★ Surely one of the most perplexing problems of life is that of grief and pain. It begins with a little child suffering perhaps pangs of hunger, the destruction of a favorite toy, or the death of a pet. Then as we reach adulthood we become familiar with pain. The physical pains we can bear much more readily than others: such as, children that become

[1] "Christ Our Example in Suffering" by James Montgomery.

more unlovely as they grow older, dreams that remain dreams only, noble ambitions that are never realized, distrust on the part of others, and then perhaps the greatest pain of all—when we ourselves become guilty of something so low, so despicable, in deed, word, or thought that we must turn into the darkness and shed bitter tears of shame. Even if no one else knows, we know; and the One on the Cross knows. One does not have to live very long to know that the road from the cradle to the grave is ofttimes soaked with tears. We wonder why. Why couldn't life be just one pleasant journey from time to eternity?

In answer to that question I would like to take you this afternoon with me back some two thousand years in time and six thousand miles in space. It is on a Friday morning at approximately 8 o'clock, and one of the sorriest processions this world has ever seen is slowly wending its way through the narrow streets of Jerusalem headed for a mound shaped like a skull outside of the gates. As the people arose that morning and girded themselves for the celebration of the Passover, they were convinced that it was all over now. This strange new religion which had caught their imagination, only a few days before as a matter of fact, was ended now—all was in defeat. Oh, true, there were some apostles who had preached, there were some sick who had been healed, many hungry had been fed—yes, even the dead had been raised—but that was passed now. They were leading him out to die, and he was going out all alone. From Bethlehem, where the angels had announced his birth to which wise men had come great distances to pay homage to him, none came to walk with him. From Nazareth, where he had spent nigh onto thirty years, no one came to console him. From Canaan, where he had gladdened the heart of a bride and graced both her home and her wedding with his presence, no bridegroom came to thank him, and so he walked alone.

Alone? Not exactly, for in Luke's Gospel we read just this one verse: "As they lead Him away, they laid hold upon one Simon, a Cyrenian, coming out of the country, and on him they laid the cross, that he might bear it after Jesus." Up the dusty road from Jordan, from the sunny shores of Africa came Simon the Cyrenian on a vacation. He was coming to Jerusalem to celebrate the Passover. Then he was going to enjoy himself. As he came within the gates of the city he saw this strange procession coming and, as anyone would have done, stopped and viewed it out of curiosity. All of a sudden the soldiers, who wanted to get about this business, who had a carpenter from Nazareth too weak to carry his cross, having stumbled and fallen several times, grabbed Simon and laid upon him the cross. Protest? Of course he protested! "I am not one of these people. I didn't have a part in the accusation. I am on vacation. I've come up here to celebrate the Passover!" He had innumerable reasons why this indignity should not be performed upon him. It did him no good. He was roughly seized and the cross placed upon his back. It was a huge cross made of rough-hewn timber, made for the purpose of holding a man until he slowly expired and died. The bitter shouts of the blood-thirsty mob that followed were no more bitter than the thoughts that went through Simon's heart. A man on a vacation made to go the way of the Cross. But as he followed that lonely figure who preceded him, because of the manner in which the cross was placed upon his shoulders, he had no alternative but to look straight ahead. Suddenly his vision began to clear. God had picked him up from the sunny shores of Africa and placed him here, at this moment, for this purpose, in order that he might be alone with Jesus Christ his Saviour. And the way of the Cross became the way of discipleship.

God is still doing that today. In our unseeing and ofttimes mad rush for wealth, power, friends that we may entertain and that we may be entertained by, fame, whatever it is that we need to satisfy our own needs, some form of pleasure in some way or another, God still reaches down from heaven and places the Cross upon our shoulders. He literally breaks our lives in two in order that he may make them whole again. He dims our eyes with tears that we may see Jesus more clearly.

Let me illustrate how he does this: The story is told of a man who had admonished his son for repeatedly disobeying him and finally said to him, "Son, if you do that once more you are going up in the attic without your dinner and spend the night." The son dared his father and the father carried out this threat. He gave his son a glass of water and a piece of bread and sent him up to the attic. When dinner was served the father sat idly toying with his food, unable to eat. His wife said to him, "John, I know what you are thinking but you can't change it now. It will spoil everything—there is nothing you can do about it." The father said, "There is something I can do about it." With that he got up, took a glass of water and a piece of bread and joined his son in the attic, and the boy spent the most memorable night of his life with his head upon his father's shoulder. In this manner God would deal with you and me when the trials and tribulations of life descend upon us. He doesn't do it inevitably, it doesn't follow automatically; but he does offer to share those dark moments with you and me if we will but let him in. Thus those dark moments of life can and will become the most glorious of all our days—filled with the sure knowledge of his love, his forgiveness, and the light of his peace.

It's the way of the Cross for us, even as it was for Simon. Thus if you will bear your crosses in that light, you will join that vast invisible army that has marched through life to eternal glory.

> To the old rugged cross I will ever be true,
> Its shame and reproach gladly bear;
> Then He'll call me some day to my home far away,
> Where His glory forever I'll share.
> So I'll cherish the old rugged cross,
> Till my trophies at last I lay down;
> I will cling to the old rugged cross,
> And exchange it someday for a crown.[2]

May God grant that to each of us. Amen.

[2] By George Bennard. Copyright renewal 1941. Homer Rodeheaver, Owner. Used by permission.

Faith and Force

OSWALD C. J. HOFFMANN

☆ ☆ ☆ We find these words in the second chapter of the First Epistle of Peter, beginning with the thirteenth verse:

Submit yourselves to every human institution for the sake of the Lord, whether to the sovereign as supreme, or to the governor as his deputy for the punishment of criminals and the commendation of those who do right. For it is the will of God that by your good conduct you should put ignorance and stupidity to silence.

Live as free men; not however as though your freedom were there to provide a screen for wrongdoing, but as slaves in God's service. Give due honor to everyone: love to the brotherhood, reverence to God, honor to the sovereign. (NEB.)

It is distinctive of our country that we have developed a relationship in which church and state can co-operate without the one dominating the life of the other: government not dictating to the church; and the church, on the other hand, not dictating to government.

This text makes it quite clear that the Word of God is down to earth. We have a down-to-earth Bible. It presents a down-to-earth Saviour who became a man like us, living as a man and dying as a man for us. Because he was a dutiful Son of his Father, he was raised from the dead by the glory of his Father to become the living Lord of heaven and of earth. The Bible offers us a down-to-earth faith in him, and it calls us to down-to-earth living. This is language we can understand! Honor everyone, love the brotherhood, by your good conduct make it evident what kind of people you are. It is the will of God that by your good conduct you should put ignorance and stupidity to silence.

We all have down-to-earth problems to deal with every day in whatever area we may find ourselves, but they may be the kind of problems that take some of us to the far corners of the earth. Indeed, the thoughts of some of us in our ordinary work are winging into outer space. This is the down-to-earth life of today! We live in a world where the X-15 has traveled at over four thousand miles per hour under the guidance of Air Force Major Robert White. I suppose during the time it would take me to say these few words, that plane would just about have made the trip from Washington to New York. We have discoverers out in space, one of which, sent up in July, took pictures in September of Hurricane Esther. The hurricane had not been detected either by aircraft or by radar. We have a Tyros IV up there which has proved that the ionosphere extends out about two thousand miles, one thousand five hundred miles farther than anyone thought before the time of the Tyros. I am very conscious of space; I speak on the radio every week and I know that radio depends on the ionosphere. Through atomic tests, we have discovered that an explosion away out there can have a great effect on the ionosphere and therefore upon radio transmission.

It is not surprising, is it, that in a world like this people should arise who claim to know everything? One of our problems in the world today is that we have to live with people who can claim to know everything. They claim to know everything that happened in the past and they also claim to know what is going to happen in the future. This is the most characteristic element in communism. The Marxist theory is a theory of history. Claiming to understand everything that happened in the past, Marxists feel they are able to tell us everything that is going to happen in the future and are absolutely sure that they are right.

The apostles of Christ who went out into the world didn't claim to know everything. But they knew one thing. They knew that Christ had come; they knew that he lives and is Lord; and they put themselves under his Lordship, recognizing that his Lordship called for down-to-earth, everyday living in faith.

They saw in government an institution of God, operating by law—law with validity based upon the universal law God himself has established. God beckons with his finger, and the planets fly in orbits dictated by him. He doesn't dictate to us but his law exists for us just the same. Government is a divine instrument to deal by just law with the willfulness and the selfishness of men. The fact that men do not observe that law does not mean that it is of no effect. It is still in existence. We in America recognize just law as a part of the divine order. I trust that we will continue to recognize this in the future.

There is no escaping the fact that law depends upon force. The Bible is not a sentimental book; it makes quite clear that the business of government is to punish criminals and to commend those who do right. That is what this text says. I've noticed that when I drive up to a stop sign and there is a policeman standing there on the corner, I'm pretty careful to come to a full stop before I start out again. A rolling stop doesn't go under those circumstances. Why? Because a certain amount of force is evident. It doesn't have to be exerted, but it is there. The law depends upon that restraint. Living in New York as I do, I am very conscious of the fact that the New Jersey drivers do not pay as much attention to the laws of our city as do the citizens who live in the city. They have the feeling, I suspect, that they are just a little bit beyond the long arm of the law; that even if they do get a ticket, maybe they won't have to pay the penalty.

The law depends upon restraint by force. This is true at home and it's true abroad. Sad, but true; that's the way the world is. I am appalled to see that when a disaster occurs in our country you almost always have to make immediate provisions against looting. When people are in the utmost misery, there are other people who will take advantage of the situation for their own purposes. Almost immediately you have to move the National Guard in and take drastic measures to prevent that sort of thing.

This happens on the domestic scene, and it happens on the international scene. There is an international confidence man operating in Moscow trying to subvert good order all over the world, ready to take whatever he can for his own selfish purpose. If we have to restrain people by force at home, we have to restrain them the same way abroad. That is the reason we have the armed forces. I dare say there are more secrets in the Pentagon than there are any other place in the world, including the Kremlin. Why? It is the nerve center of the greatest military machine that has ever been gathered in the history of the world. Why? Because of the kind of world in which we live.

The Bible makes no bones about what kind of a world it is. We would like to tell things that are pleasant to people. But the Bible can't tell things that are pleasant when the facts are unpleasant. A doctor hates to tell a man that the x-ray shows a malignancy; he would rather say that there is nothing wrong at all. It is tough to have to tell people that things are wrong.

It was tough for the Lord Jesus Christ to say to people that the imagination of man's heart is evil from his youth. But it's a fact. We are part of this world and a part of mankind. If government has been set up to control people from without, God has his own way of controlling people from within. He sent his own Son to be a man, to live our life, and to endure the destiny of death for us. I invite you to believe this is true, that it really happened, that God has taken a hand in human history in the person of his Son and that he has a cure for each of you.

We have national and international problems. I know that you have domestic and personal problems. God is interested in all of them, either through the instrumentality of government or through redemption of the individual. He wants people to work with a good conscience knowing that they belong to him and are his children by faith in the Lord Jesus Christ.

Is there a place for a Christian soldier in this world of ours? There certainly is. The Bible is not a pacifist book. It doesn't encourage saber-rattling purely for selfish purposes, either on the part of individuals or of government, nor does it ask that we stand idly by while nations are being devastated any more than it asks that we stand by if our wives are being violated and our children murdered before our eyes.

The Bible understands men, how they are made; that is why Christ had to come. Why he had to die—for all of us. And why he lives as the Lord of heaven and of earth! We are the children of God, if we believe and trust and follow Jesus Christ. I call upon you in this great place to be a leaven for Jesus Christ, remembering him, looking unto him, and being the kind of people who are inspired by the faith and love of Jesus Christ, of which our Bible says that "[love] never faileth: but whether there be prophesies, they shall fail; whether there be tongues, they shall cease; whether there be knowledge, it shall vanish away. For we know in part, and we prophesy in part. But when that which is perfect is come, then that which is in part shall be done away." We can be that kind of people right here and now.

Let us pray: God give us that kind of faith and love in Christ. Help our country to be the kind of country that is on your side, depending on your help and guidance, direction and protection. Amen.

Begin Where You Are

PAUL S. REES

⭐⭐⭐ If in the calendar of the Christian year Christmas is the Festival of Love, and Good Friday is the Festival of Mercy, and Easter is the Festival of Life, then surely Pentecost is the Festival of Power. I take you now to an Old Testament story in which we have a kind of preview of how the Holy Spirit gives to men the power for living which they so acutely need.

Six centuries befores Christ the fortunes of the people of Judah and Jerusalem were at low ebb. A flood of judgment—the Chaldean invasion —had washed them out of their land and stranded them as exiles in Babylon.

Among the thousands of captives taken by Nebuchadnezzar's army was a young man of not more than twenty-five, perhaps less, who bore the name of Ezekiel. A married man, he managed somehow to get housed in comparative comfort in a district somewhat removed from the masses of his fellow countrymen.

Several years went by—probably about five—and this young husband began to receive visitors from among the exiled Jews. They were "elders" who wanted some word from the young prophet as to what would be the fate of the city of Jerusalem, which they had been forced to evacuate.

Jerusalem, it should be remembered, was not destroyed by the men of Babylon until 586 B.C., eleven years after the great deportation.

The coming of these elders, with their pressing questions, meant that a job was cut out for Ezekiel which was by no means easy. Here they were—prophet and people alike—caught in the same net. They had lost their homes, their country, their Temple, their national independence.

And now God is about to assign Ezekiel the task of telling his people that before things get better they are going to get worse. This was the dark and dismaying situation in the midst of which God said to his young servant, "All right, Ezekiel, get to your feet. There's a job to be done. Let's get on with it."

And get on with it Ezekiel did! Indeed, as we all know, he became one of the greatest of the Hebrew prophets. In telling about his experience he says, "The spirit entered into me . . . and set me upon my feet."

Beginning where he was—in exile, humiliation, and weakness—he moved out to ventures so bold and achievements so notable that his name ranks high among the prophetic immortals.

In all of this I see something that I need for myself. I suspect that some of you need it too. There's a job to be done. There's a duty to be performed. There's a dream to be converted into reality. There's a habit to be broken and a better one put in its place. There's a character to be transformed. There's a weakness to be overcome.

But where to begin?

Haven't we all faced it? And there's something by way of an answer here in this bracing story of Ezekiel: Begin where you are.

I

Begin, as I imagine this man had to begin, with some *basic recognitions*. There's the important recognition, for example, that *wherever God speaks to a man that place becomes, then and there, sacredly and even excitingly meaningful*.

Ezekiel found that even Babylon can become a listening post whereat the voice of God is heard.

Or think of Moses. In one verse we read that "he led the flock to the backside of the desert." "The desert!" mind you. But in the next verse we read: "And the angel of the Lord appeared unto him in a flame of fire out of the midst of a bush." Three verses later we learn that Moses heard the Divine Voice saying, "The place whereon thou standest is holy ground."

Right here where you are, Moses, where now I am speaking to you— this is holy ground. Temples and churches are excellent places to meet God, but they are not the *only* places. Wherever God can find a sensitive, listening, worshiping man he can turn even an acacia bush into a cathedral.

Or think of a modern instance of hearing the voice of God in a strange and unpromising place. The name of Wilfred Grenfell is forever associated with Christian missions in Labrador. But how many of us know that when he first visited that bleak, frozen Labrador coast it was for the purpose of a vacation cruise? It was to be a holiday for the doctor. Afterwards he wrote: "I attended nine hundred persons who never would have seen a doctor if I had not been there." Thus it was that in the midst of the stinging cold and the appalling ignorance and the wasting diseases of those Labrador people the man who had come there for a holiday adventure heard the voice of God, calling him to devote his life to a population whom modern medicine and missions had forgotten.

Yes, whether it be the hot sands of the Arabian desert or the frozen wastes of the Labrador shore, even there God speaks. Even there one can find the beginnings of great things. This we must recognize.

But there's another thing: We must recognize that beginning where we are means tackling ourselves. If you think that is dead easy, just try it.

If there's a task to be performed, a problem to be solved, a mess to be cleaned up, we usually begin by trying to pin the responsibility on someone else. Or, if not that, by plunging headlong into the business at hand, with little regard for the question of whether or not we are fit to do anything or go anywhere.

Take it in Ezekiel's case. Before he was ready to begin the prophetic ministry that was to be his in Babylon, before he was permitted to answer the questions put to him by these elders among the Jewish captives, he did a very strange thing.

He moved out from the relative comfort of his little house and went down by the river bank where a multitude of these exiles were having a rough time of it. In telling about it later he says, "I sat where they sat," just sharing their lonely, melancholy lot and getting the "feel" of their wretchedness!

The late M. S. Rice of Detroit was in another city one stiflingly hot summer night. He was to address a large convention. Starting early from his hotel, his thought was to go without dinner but to stop at a soft drink counter and get a cold glass of orange juice. Just as he was lifting the glass to his lips he felt a touch on his arm and, looking down, he saw there a little, withered, ragged Negro woman, who said appealingly, "Mister, I'm thirsty too!"

In the circumstances, said Dr. Rice, she had me. Shakespeare couldn't have been more skillful with words than she was in the simple use of that little word "too." Had she said only, "I am thirsty," it would not have had half the appeal that was packed into that little syllable "too." He saw to it that she got the biggest glass of orange juice she had drunk in a long time. Recalling the incident later, he said, "What right had I to indulge my own thirst when here beside me stood a thirsty one with nothing with which to meet the fact?"

II

Let's carry this thought of starting where you are a little further. In addition to some basic recognitions, we need to begin with some *bold responses*.

Right where you are, start being a listener among the listless. Ezekiel did. "Son of man, stand upon thy feet, and I will speak unto thee." Remember that no one thought of young Ezekiel as a mighty prophet at that time. His reputation for greatness came centuries afterward. He was an ordinary man who was willing to be quiet long enough for God to speak to him.

Begin now, and let me join you in it, to spend less time offering words to God in prayer and more time listening for the Word of God to come through to you. Not long ago, in the midst of a busy day, I found about five things swiftly converging on me, demanding my attention at the same time. Suddenly I felt things getting tight within. I recognized it as a bad symptom. Having learned not to ignore the danger signal, I inwardly prayed for poise. In less time than I can tell it, the Inner Voice spoke in the language of Scripture, "He giveth quietness." Others will have to speak for themselves. I can only say that I found it more effective than I suspect it would have been if I had seized a pill box and swallowed a tranquilizer!

God fills the air with his messages. But, as in the case of radio and television, you don't get them unless you "tune in."

Or again, right where you are, start being *a speaker among the silent*. That's what Ezekiel had to do. "Thou shalt speak my words unto them, whether they will hear, or whether they will forbear." In American Christianity today we have millions of members who are vocal—and even excited—on every subject under the sun except the subject of Jesus Christ and their faith in him.

P. W. Philpott used to tell of a New York pastor who laid a plea for personal witnessing before his Board of Elders. Next day one of these elders, a prominent businessman, called a male secretary into his private office, and asked:

"John, how long have you been here?"

"Five years."

"Do you know that I'm a Christian?"

"Yes, sir."

"Do you know I'm an elder in the church?"

"Yes, sir. I've been in your church."

"John, are you a Christian?"

"No, sir."

"Have you ever wondered that I have not asked you about this before?"

"Yes, sir, I have. When I first came here, I expected that you would talk to me about it, but you didn't."

At this, the man arose, extended his hand, and said, "John, forget my position now. I'm just a man, full of faults and weaknesses. Will you forgive me? Will you kneel down here and pray with me this morning?"

John did kneel. John did pray. He prayed not only for his employer but for himself. That was the morning of John's conversion.

It was the morning, let it be added, that this Presbyterian elder began where he was, right there in his office, to be a speaker for Christ among the silent.

You see it's the immediate and decisive response for which God is asking. There are other responses, to be sure, besides these I have urged. You can begin where you are to be *courageous* among the fearful. You can begin where you are to be *tolerant* among the fierce and intolerant. You can start where you are to be *faithful* among the faithless.

The point is: Let's get on with it!

III

There's one thing more. Start with some basic recognitions? Yes. And with some bold responses? Yes. But, whatever you do, don't fail to start with some *bountiful resources*.

These resources are not of your contriving; they are of God's giving. Mark well the connection between the first verse of the second chapter of Ezekiel, which is our text, and the second verse: "Son of man, stand upon your feet. . . . And . . . the Spirit entered into me and set me upon my feet" (RSV).

Here, I am persuaded, the translators of the Revised Standard Version have put us in their debt by taking the word "spirit," spelled with a small "s" in the King James Version, and making it a capital "S." It is indeed the Spirit of God who invaded and possessed and enabled Ezekiel. In the following chapter, this is even more emphatic. Twice over the prophet says, "The Spirit lifted me up."

"Your brain," an old English schoolmaster used to say, "should not be a cold-storage chamber but a powerhouse." I suggest that in a deeper, bigger sense this is true of the soul. It is never God's intention that the soul should be a kind of cold-storage room where our religious ideals and beliefs are properly sorted, protected, and preserved but a powerhouse where energies are generated and released for the day-by-day business of vital and victorious living. It is precisely at this point that the Holy Spirit works the miracle of his power in our surrendered lives.

Begin where you are to be not a generator of power but a receiver of power. By surrender and faith you become a channel, open and usable, through which God-power, the power of the Holy Spirit, begins to operate.

At the close of a spiritual life retreat a Christian, who had been living a defeated life, arose and said: "I've been inspired and enlightened before, but this time I've been cleansed."

Who can do that but the Holy Spirit? Who can take the power of

Christ's cross, the holy energy of his blood and release it at the deepest levels of our inner life for the purifying and unifying of our divided, defeated personality—who but the Holy Spirit?

"Strengthened with might by his Spirit in the inner man," is Paul's way of saying it in Eph. 3:16.

Psychology can examine, philosophy can explore, morality can entreat, theology can explain, ritual can enamour, but it takes the Holy Spirit to *empower*.

Begin where you are! Not by flexing your weary muscles or blowing on your hands or gritting your teeth—not this self-effort.

Begin by opening up to resources that are infinitely beyond you but which, thanks to the ministry of the Holy Spirit, will be released with you —vitally, triumphantly.

Freedom's Underwriters

WALTER H. JUDD

★ ★ ☆ The Fourth of July is the most uniquely American holiday because it is the birthday of our country. But it's more than that. Our Independence Day is the birthday of genuine political freedom around the world.

Like all birthdays, it is a time for us to rejoice over our glorious past. It is also a time for us to take a good look at our disturbed present and to take our bearings for the future. How are things going in our country and in our world on this birthday?

If one word were to describe our country's mood today it would probably be "confusion." Never has any people had so much to be grateful for, and I think never has any people been more deeply thankful for the goodness of life that is possible for us in this blessed land. We are free! One-third of the people of the world today are denied even the opportunity to attend a worship service of their choice. We have plenty to eat at a time when so many in other parts of the world never have enough.

Yet I dare say that never has there been a time in our country's history characterized by greater uneasiness, uncertainty, perplexity, dismay. Here it is seventeen years after we won a war with the unconditional surrender of all our enemies; we had every advantage, and we yet find ourselves soberly asking, How can we survive? Can Korea go on indefinitely artificially divided, half Communist, half free? Or Germany? Or Europe? Can this contracted planet go on indefinitely with almost one-half of its people denied freedom, and we be secure in a sort of charmed life here? Down deep inside, I think we realize the answer is no. But we don't quite know what to do about it.

We rejoice that no such things happen to people here as we have seen happen in Hungary and Tibet and, closer home, in Cuba. But no American is easy in his mind that such things can be happening to people anywhere right here in the middle of the supposedly enlightened and emancipated twentieth century.

Perhaps the major reason for our confusion and uncertainty is that we have not fully understood the nature of the struggle dividing our world. We know it's a conflict of arms. We dare not fall behind; else the other side could say to us, Surrender or perish.

We know it is a conflict of economic systems. Which will crack up first under the awful load? If we don't spend more for arms, we invite insecurity—and disaster. If we do spend more and more for arms and for everything else that we want, we invite a weakening of our economy—and disaster. Either way, disaster. This is why Mr. Khrushchev smiles when he says, "We will bury you!" He is convinced that we are so intent on comforts and pleasures right now that we won't be willing to discipline ourselves to put first things first.

Fewer see that it is also a conflict of educational systems. Which will produce not only the smartest but the toughest minds? I have frequently told of a high school in my city of Minneapolis whose top five honor students in the graduating class three years ago had all come to this country since the end of the war as the children of displaced persons. Did they have higher IQ's than our native-born Minnesota youngsters, mostly Scandinavian in ancestry? Of course not. The DP children appreciated their opportunity in this blessed land and worked harder.

Many have not seen that the conflict is still deeper. It is a conflict between two totally different philosophies of life and, therefore, of government. It is a conflict between two totally different sets of values, two different ways of looking at things; and that means between two different concepts as to the nature of man, two different concepts as to the nature of the universe, two different concepts as to the nature of God—or whether God is.

Charles Malik, the Christian Lebanese philosopher who was President of the United Nations General Assembly a few years ago, has said that when the Conference on Human Rights met in Paris after World War II to work out and proclaim a Universal Declaration of Human Rights they spent months trying, in vain, to agree on what a human being is. How do you determine and declare the rights to which a human being is by nature entitled if you don't agree on what his nature is? One side believes that every man is a child of God, created by a Creator, and endowed by that Creator with certain inalienable rights—born with them. Man was created, as the Scripture puts it, in the image and likeness of God, which means that he has not just a larger and smarter brain than other animals; he has something of the Divine in him, something that enables him to sense moral values, a capacity to make moral judgments, and to make independent decisions, yes or no, on the basis of those judgments. Such an estimate of the nature of man was the foundation on which this nation was established on that first Independence Day.

But the Communists say there is no God and no moral order in the universe, so man has no such inherent, inalienable rights. The great Russian scientist, Dr. Pavlov, demonstrated that he could take young dogs away from old dogs before the old dogs had had a chance to teach them their habits and, by rigidly controlling the environment of the young dogs, he could produce, within narrow limits fortunately, the reactions he wanted: predictable, unvarying, automatic reactions from the dogs. The Communists say this can be done with man and they intend to do it.

I was in an area in South China under the control of the Chinese Communists for eight months in 1930 and again in North China for about five months in 1937 and 1938. I have spent hours listening to these doctrines. They are no secret. They say that you and I think we have the capacity to make moral judgments because all these centuries we have been told so by rabbis, priests, ministers, and writers of Declarations of

Independence, but that we really don't have such a capacity—we aren't born that way. If we had not been conditioned by these ideas, communicated to us in our formative years, then we wouldn't even think we have the capacity to make moral judgments.

So this world conflict is not an old-fashioned effort like those of Caesar, Napoleon, Alexander the Great, even Hitler, to seize other people's territory or gold or slaves. This is a struggle about the nature of man. Is there or is there not a moral order in the universe? Are there or are there not moral laws in the universe which, like the physical laws of gravity and electricity, man can violate but cannot break? The Communists say there is no such moral order; it's a myth, a superstition, and it's their mission to "liberate" us from such old notions that imprison our minds. For the first time in centuries our civilization is challenged by a passionately missionary competitor, striking not at just the result of the ideas and faith proclaimed in the Declaration of Independence, which is our country today, but at the very ideas and faith themselves.

This is why we haven't been able to get any real agreement with the Soviet Union, whether at Yalta or Potsdam, the United Nations or Geneva —however hard our efforts or far-reaching our concessions. They are not pursuing the same objectives as we. We want a settlement; they want conquest. We want to end the struggle; they intend to win it. When they come to a conference, it isn't to remove misunderstandings and improve relations, it's to take our temperature and find the best ways to take us in.

And why are they not pursuing the same objectives as we? Because they don't believe the same things we believe—about man, about the universe, about God.

So a main reason why we are in trouble is because we haven't studied thoroughly this heresy, this disease of the mind, called communism, as doctors study tuberculosis or polio. We tend to project into the minds of Communists our religious concepts which they have rejected, and then we are upset when they don't live by these religious values. But it is both useless and absurd to denounce them for failing to safeguard the rights with which we believe man is endowed by his Creator, as long as they insist there is no Creator.

I suspect one reason we haven't fully understood the nature of this conflict and of this adversary is because we have grown fuzzy about ourselves. We have failed to understand or forgotten the essential nature of our own culture and our heritage of freedom. How did it begin? Some in Europe who had been denied the right to worship God as they pleased came to the New World determined to have religious liberty. They had discovered they could not be sure of religious liberty without political liberty. The rest of the world was ruled from the top down: by political rulers, economic rulers, religious rulers, landed gentry, aristocracies. These pilgrims had no precedent, they had no blueprint, but they had clear minds. They devised a political system under which for the first time in history on a major national scale people could control government instead of government controlling them, as was the rule in all the rest of the world then and is the rule in so much of the world today.

The system worked, because it released the creative capacities of ordinary people. In the old frozen societies, the son of a farmer automatically became a farmer, even though he had the urge and capacity to become a musician or a mathematician or a scientist, or a statesman. But here in America any boy or girl could do whatever he wanted with whatever ability, dream, urge he had. In the most unexpected places, in people from all races, classes, and climes, genius appeared. It had always been there, but until this system of government of which we are trustees came into being, it had never had such opportunity to express itself. There took place in America an almost unbelievable outburst of creative imagination, invention, effort, production. Thus were our progress and wealth achieved.

And then what happened? We became so enamored with the material results that many forgot about the spiritual causes. Family worship began to die out. People paid less and less attention to the Holy Scriptures, and then less and less attention to the principles revealed in them. They began to think they could get good by doing evil, justice by bowing down before injustice, freedom by accepting enslavement of other peoples—as if man, created in the likeness of God and born to be free, can ever be content or "better off" just because somebody is taking care of his physical needs, like a steer in a feed pen. Some in America came to believe we can get trust by being untrustworthy or treat other peoples with condescension and still have their confidence and goodwill. Thus did we come to our present confusion and uncertainty.

What must we do now? It seems to me the answer is clear. We have to go back to where we got off the track, as the way to go forward again. We have to rediscover the essence of our heritage, the faith that gave our country its birth. We must revitalize devotion to the principles from which came the rights we have enjoyed. The government's proper role is not to manage our lives but to secure for us those rights.

This means first of all we have to recapture our faith. Our faith is that God *is*. If God is not, then of all people in the world we are the most foolish. Our effort is bound to fail. If we do not have as our Father a God who created all men as his children, then we are not brothers; and it's silly sentimentality to talk about the brotherhood of man. But if God is, then what ought to be can be, and there is no reason for anxiety. There are long, hard, dark valleys to go through but no justification for despair. Our faith also is that God is available to every man. We can know his will; we can have access to his power—if we will seek him.

Second, we have to rediscover the essential principles. They are in our history books, but supremely in the Scriptures that inspired and guided our fathers. One cannot become a good surgeon without long study of his surgery books. No one becomes a good general or admiral without years at the academies and of continuing study. It is surprising that so many are confused about the principles essential to a free society when they don't take time to study the "textbook" where the principles are set forth.

We have to be willing to take these principles right down into everyday life and put them into practice in our work, in our homes, in our clubs, in our responsibilities as citizens. We have to apply the principles as well as know them.

Lastly, we have to rediscover and emulate the great prophets and leaders of freedom, those who perceived the essential realities and showed how to build on them a great nation. For those of us who are Christians, it means we have to rediscover and rededicate ourselves to that Leader whom we call Lord and Master.

I have been recommending a book which someone sent me called *They Signed for Us*. It's just a thumbnail sketch of the fifty-six men who signed the Declaration of Independence 186 years ago. I learned a lot that I had forgotten or had never known. I had forgotten that they didn't sign it on the Fourth of July; they only voted to sign it and then got out of town because now they were traitors. There was a price of five hundred pounds on the heads of John Hancock and John Adams, a small fortune in those days. They signed it a month later on August 2. Their names were not made public for six months longer in the hope that they could get back safely to their homes, all the way from New Hampshire to Georgia. Some of them never got back during all the years of the war.

Do you remember what they wrote? *"For the support of this declaration, with firm reliance on the protection of Divine Providence, we mutually pledge to each other our lives,"*—I had forgotten how many gave their lives. One who lived in New Jersey found when he got home that his wife and some of his children had been seized by the British and thrown into a dungeon. He himself did not live through the war. *"Our fortunes,"*—I had never known how many gave their fortunes. For example, the four who signed from New York were all very wealthy. Two had fleets of ocean-sailing vessels. They lost everything. All four died in straitened circumstances. *"and our sacred honor."*—not a man wavered.

They signed for us. The time has come when we must start signing for ourselves.

In Such an Age

FREDERICK BROWN HARRIS

☆ ☆ ☆ Independence Day is one of our best-loved national days. It is the day that symbolizes our great love for freedom. On the Fourth of July we annually commemorate our national independence, but it is also a day of commitment. For while we gaze with gratitude and gain inspiration and courage, as we remember old, unhappy, far-off days and battles long ago, we know that in any journey to the yesterdays, we must be sure to have a two-way ticket and return to the present in which we live. It is ours not simply to revel in the past, no matter how glorious, but to serve the present day.

When he was a very popular preacher—a long time ago now—and everybody was talking about evolution, T. de Witt Talmage began a sermon with this sentence: "If we leave it to the evolutionists to tell us where we came from and to the theologians to tell us where we are going, the fact still remains that we are here." It is that solemn realization that is expressed in Harry Emerson Fosdick's great hymn, "God of Grace and God of Glory." Some time ago, I heard ten thousand people sing it with Dr. Fosdick standing there on the platform. It contains this petition:

Grant us wisdom,
Grant us courage,
For the facing of this hour,

.   .   .   .   .

For the living of these days.[1]

It is the thrill and challenge of this hour and of this age which sings
in Angela Morgan's lilting lines:

To be alive in such an age!
With every year a lightning page
Turned in the world's great wonder book

.   .   .   .   .   .

When steel and stone and rail and rod
Become the avenue of God—
A trump to shout His thunder through
To crown the work that man may do.

.   .   .   .   .   .

O age of strife!
O age of life!

.   .   .   .   .   .

To be alive in such an age—

.   .   .   .   .   .

Rise, soul, from thy despairing knees.

.   .   .   .   .   .

Give thanks with all thy flaming heart—
Crave but to have in it a part.
Give thanks and clasp thy heritage—
To be alive in such an age! [2]

Now, if with but a handful of words, we should undertake to analyze
such an age—our age—apart from the fact that it is the age of the split
atom with all the dread implications of that discovery, we would have
to say, wouldn't we, that this is a time of world revolution. The headlines
of today's papers shout that! That means that teeming millions, under
all skies—especially under Asian and African skies—are reaching out,

---

[1] Used by permission.
[2] "To-day." Used by permission of Dodd, Mead & Company, Inc.

often violently, and demanding angrily more of the good things that modern civilization has made possible. We do not regret that. America at its best has nothing that it does not desire for all mankind. What we call the world revolution is largely the harvest of the seeds of democracy and Christianity.

But, side by side with this, we see a heinous system of chains and enslavement which is endeavoring to pervert and utilize that legitimate revolution for its own evil ends. It is a system which, like vultures, hovers over the misery of the world. It is a conspiracy against decency, with no belief in God, kindness, fairness, mercy, truth, or what we think of as moral standards. It defies and denies and derides all that we hold dear.

For the first time in history we are fronting a terrible enemy who blasphemes the very basis of our life, debases the dignity of man, and desecrates the beliefs by which we live. Sometime ago my good friend, Gerald Kennedy, a bishop of The Methodist Church, whose prophetic voice is heard in all the land, spent some weeks in Soviet Russia. He is a liberal in much of his social thinking, and we wondered what he would say after he had had the opportunity at firsthand to see the good and the bad in the system which holds sway behind the Iron Curtain. Coming back to this land of liberty where he could breathe free once more, this is his verdict: "The issue is joined at last, either God is or he is not. Either a man is of value only as a citizen of the state, or he is of value because God created him. Either Christianity is true or communism is true, but not both." Then this dynamic American leader added, "Co-existence is a pleasant term, but one of these systems is going down."

It is of that system that the late Senator Vandenberg used to say, "Appeasement is surrender on the installment plan." But not long ago a woman who was obsessed by the objectives of some questionable peace crusade, said to me, "Why can't we all simply talk of nothing but peace, just as the Russians seem to be?" Said she, "Don't you believe that the time will come when the old Bible prophecy will be fulfilled, and the lion and the lamb shall lie down together?" "Yes," I said, "we must all hope for that consummation, and toil ardently that it may come to pass. But when it does, and the lion and the lamb lie down together, we want to be mighty sure that the lamb will not be inside the lion."

And so in such an age we desperately need new Paul Reveres to ride up and down the lanes and roads of America's pleasant prosperity, reminding us in season and out of season that eternal vigilance is still the price of liberty and that our heritage is not just an heirloom to be handed down as a cherished gem to the generations following—it is something that must be relived, reinterpreted, and rewon with every new generation. It is, therefore, for us wherever we stand, and whatever we do, to give the best that is in us.

> For the cause that lacks assistance,
> For the wrong that needs resistance,
> For the future in the distance,
>   And the good that I can do.[8]

It is intensely interesting and significant to read the labels that the contemporaries of each century have pasted upon the gateposts of their times. The prophets of Israel were nearly all past masters at coining dismal labels for their particular day as they thundered their warnings. For instance, in reading Isaiah recently I noticed that he declared that his age was a time of "darkness and sorrow." Strange to say, that is about the same label that leaders in every century including our own have suggested characterizes their own time. And what those whom we call the founding fathers had to say about the present and future prospects of democracy, as they stood about the cradle of our state, often did not sound exactly like a jubilate!

A way back in the days when I was in college Henry van Dyke wrote a little book which he called *The Gospel for an Age of Doubt.* That, you see, was his "label" for that day all those years ago!

Across the years, I've always remembered one sentence in that little book. He said: "A coat of arms for this age might well be three bishops dormant and an interrogation point rampant." Well, that would be a good coat of arms for our day, wouldn't it?

Speaking of bishops reminds me that the Episcopalians held a great conference sometime ago in Honolulu, and after the adjournment of the conclave, most of the delegates were returning home to the mainland.

[8] "What I Live For," by George Linnaeus Banks.

One plane had quite a heavy load of ecclesiastical brass. Just about half way between Honolulu and San Francisco, one motor quit—that is not as bad as two but it is bad enough—and you can imagine the whistling-in-the-dark kind of conversation that was going on. One delegate, perhaps a little more pious than some of the rest, manged to slip up to the pilot, whose face showed his concern and anxiety. Said the messenger of hope, "Don't worry about this situation, we are going to get in safely. I thought you would like to know we have eight bishops on this plane." To which, without looking up, the pilot replied, "I'd rather have four motors than eight bishops."

Well, as we stand at the wailing walls of our troubled times, they seem as full of discounting labels as the highway billboards are of screaming advertisements. In addition to the Communistic label, which is real enough, we are constantly being told that this is a time of moral sag, a time when materialism and secularism are eating out the very fiber of civilization. So read the labels in this year of our Lord! Let us admit that one does not have to be a pessimist to find plenty of black paint in the picture of America in such an age. In spite of rather rosy and often specious figures with regard to church buildings and church attendance, moral delinquency is so debauching, spiritual illiteracy is so appalling, secularism is so blighting, money poured out for strong drink and softening luxuries is such a mighty torrent, contrasted with the tiny trickle for character building enterprises, that it is no wonder a writer who is not an alarmist declared in one of our popular magazines not long ago that the symptoms in America today are ominously similar to those of Rome just before the fall.

Shall we confess that in our age the ruling passion with half our people is to build more barns and bigger barns or corporations and bigger corporations and the ruling and raging passion of the other half of our people is to get more and more wages for less and less work, no matter what it does to the rest of society. So we make wealth and security the goals of our personal living and of our national existence! The sad fact facing a materialistic society like ours is that we often have nothing to promise except more gadgets and what we call an ever higher "standard of living" or "way of life."

While in the South sometime ago, I heard of a young woman who was a teacher of political science in one of the schools down there. They were talking about a question she raised in her classroom. When someone spoke of the Russian threat to overtake us in material goods, this fine young teacher said to her class, "Suppose that in ten or fifteen years the Russians could catch up with us in the production of consumer goods, conveniences, and clever gadgets. Suppose the Soviets accomplish the gains they boast and even surpass us in mere things. What would we then have left to prove the superiority of our way, the validity of our faith?"

Constantly I get a great many books to review—more than I can even read! But one came not long ago which strangely gripped my attention and interest. It was by a newspaper reporter who had gone across the nation interviewing prominent men in various parts of America. He wanted to find out what a number of things—culture, music, books, and so on—meant in the lives of these men who, in their own cities, were thought of as outstanding. One thing he asked about was religion. He did not want to know whether or not they belonged to some fashionable place of worship or, if they did, whether they ushered or passed the plate. He wanted to know what spiritual verities really meant in their lives. What do you think he called the chapter which was a summary of his inquiries regarding religion? Its title was: "The Tyranny of Things," for he found that so many who were active in the busy affairs of the city really were groping down a narrow gorge with blinded eyes and hobbled feet and calling it "life."

So in such an age it is time to ring the Liberty Bell again! We freely confess that the hands which grasp the rope are imperfect, fallible hands. But even as we listen to the most caustic analysis of our own evils and betrayals of freedom, there is still a majestic consciousness of something lofty and holy as the bell rings out again, for it still has a creative faith to proclaim to the nations. True democracy cannot successfully confront totalitarianism unless it has a faith in spiritual verities stronger than the fanatical sophistry of Marxist materialism. John Glenn, the astronaut, has said just that in an inspiring way.

A dozen years ago a replica of the bell which proclaimed independence was fashioned in the famous Paccard foundries of France. And even in the present, unfortunate period of misunderstanding, we must never forget that France helped to ring our Liberty Bell in those dark, doubtful days of the Revolution. One of these exact reproductions of the Liberty Bell was set up on the White House grounds and was rung by the President. Its dulcet tone was a message to the world that all true Americans are sons of the Revolution. To ring that bell in 1776 was dangerous. To ring that bell today is dangerous—it is slavery that is easy and safe. Freedom is always difficult and hazardous!

> Our fathers in a wondrous age,
>   Ere yet the Earth was small,
> Ensured to us an heritage,
>   And doubted not at all
> That we, the children of their heart,
>   Which then did beat so high,
> In later time should play like part
>   For our posterity.
>
> .   .   .   .
>
> Dear-bought and clear, a thousand year,
>   Our fathers' title runs.
> Make we likewise their sacrifice,
>   Defrauding not our sons! [4]

That is a call to danger for, as children of the Revolution today, we front massed foes who repudiate the principles of our Declaration of Independence and the validity of the news of the Liberty Bell proclaims. We face those whose announced goal is the destruction of our democracy as we have known it. Now whether at any one time in their strategy the enemy frowns or smiles, is rude or courteous, friendly or hostile is not in itself relevent. Grins may be more dangerous than guns! Bouquets may be more damaging than bombs! Those who threaten us are often, to use a phrase of Shakespeare, like the smiling flower with the serpent under it. Often in these days naïve people seem to think that it is stupid to be religious, and are ready to give three cheers for every Soviet change of facial expression.

All that we mean by America started with the creed summed up in the opening sentence of the Pilgrim's Declaration when they stepped upon the rock on the wild New England shore. That sentence began, "In the

[4] "The Heritage" from *Songs from Books* by Rudyard Kipling. Used by permission of Mrs. George Bambridge and A. P. Watt & Son.

Name of God!" That is where the American dream started. It will be ended without it. We cannot beat something with nothing! Our greatest foe is a listless faith—tame, timid, and tepid—that muffles the bell! As we ring it again in this time of crises and alarm, we must match our profession with the sacred promise of Independence Hall—"We mutually pledge to each other our lives, our fortunes, and our sacred honor."

Only the reincarnation of the undimmed faith and dauntless courage, which saved us then can save us now! The Liberty Bell must be rung again!

A Nation Whose God Is the Lord

IVAN L. BENNETT

☆☆☆ "Blessed is the nation whose God is the Lord." (Ps. 33:12.) The thirty-third psalm belongs in context with a group of psalms which have something to say about the *favorable situation* of people who trust in God and keep his commandments.

The word in the Hebrew Old Testament translated in these psalms and in this text as "blessed" is *esher*. It is a strong word rarely found in the Hebrew Old Testament save in these psalms, and in the prophets Isaiah and Jeremiah. It portrays:

1. *the favorable situation* of those whose sins are forgiven, whose transgressions are removed, unto whom the Lord imputeth not iniquity.

2. *those whose defense is sure.* God is their shield and buckler, their fortress and their sure defense.

3. *those who are liberated from paralyzing fear.* These psalms came out of a background where people had much to fear, but the people portrayed in these psalms are unafraid of "the arrow that flieth by day," "the terror by night," or "the destruction that wasteth at noonday." The God of history was their refuge and their sure defense.

That, I submit, would be something for America, somewhat shaky at the knees when Mr. Khrushchev rumbles threateningly to us.

Our Fathers, Concerned with Human Liberty, Trusted in God

This nation was founded, and has developed within the framework of faith and hope in God. We sing:

> O God, beneath Thy guiding hand
> Our exiled fathers crossed the sea.

And:

> Thy love divine hath led us in the past;
> In this free land by Thee our lot is cast.

Those who promulgated the Declaration of Independence were aware of great personal responsibility and they were concerned with freedom. They pledged their lives, their fortunes, and their sacred honor, but also they acted "in firm reliance upon the protection of divine Providence." They expected to be "laborers together with God."

Those who framed the Constitution were aware that the freedom they had won must be a responsible freedom. In order to endure, it must be freedom under law. When the delegates faced up to their task, *even in the making of laws,* they were aware of the continuing need of the protection and guiding hand of divine Providence. Benjamin Franklin, calling the delegates to prayer for guidance and grace, stated that if a sparrow could not fall to the ground without the notice of our Heavenly Father, it was unlikely that the delegates assembled could succeed without his aid.

Some of us will recall the charge given by General Pershing to the forces under his command in France: "Hardship will be your lot, but trust in God, who will give you comfort."

The Promise to the Responsible

The promise of this fortunate situation is not to the coward or to the mollycoddle. In New England there was public thanksgiving for a repast consisting of clams and bread made of Indian corn. But it was understood that those who did not work could not eat. Nor did they see any inconsistency in praying, "Give us this day our daily bread."

The writers of the Constitution, believing that without divine assistance they would not succeed, saw no inconsistency in writing into that document that the Congress should provide for the national defense.

It was only five years after the adoption of this organic law, conceived in the framework of the citizens as laborers together with God in the building of a nation, that William Carey launched the modern missionary movement, challenging the men of the church to work in a like framework, saying, "Attempt great things for God. Expect great things from God."

While we cannot in the present situation of our world eschew the dreaded possibility of the need to use force and to risk our lives in using it, we know that it has been demonstrated in history that God does not choose sides on the basis of the largest battalions. Victory has too often been on the side of the small battalions plus the right.

Some Essential Disciplines

This text is of universal application, but it must be obvious to everyone that our beloved country as a nation under God stands in need of some disciplines.

For one thing, there is a need for *a fuller grasp of the Christian concept of human dignity* in this generation that has witnessed so great manifestation of human depravity. On that depravity there is no need to elaborate. Some of you have seen Buchenwald; many of you have seen Dachau and Camp O'Donnell. None of us has escaped the dismay that comes with the cheapness with which human life is regarded in America today.

A few weeks ago a recorded interview with a noted mathematician was featured on one of our local TV stations. The interviewer made it clear that he regards the gentleman as "one of the great philosophers of all time." In any evaluation of his philosophy, his definition of *humanity* must be remembered. He once called it "a small but boisterous bit of organic scum which for the time being inhabits one of the smaller planets." That, I submit, is not fit to live by.

If humanity is organic scum then humanity with impunity may

behave as organic scum, but you cannot sustain a system of free government which is based on the sovereignty of the people when people behave like that.

If people are organic scum then the slave drivers, the Hitlers, the Tojos, the Eichmanns, and the Quislings may with impunity treat people as organic scum, but you cannot have decency in human relations when people are treated as organic scum. But if, as our founding fathers believed and as our Bible teaches, people bear the image of their Maker, and have the potential for redemption so that they become members of the household of faith and heirs of God and joint heirs with Jesus Christ, then there is a law of human relations resting upon the absolutes of the unchanging nature of God. Centuries of Western civilization have demonstrated that good government (and moral order) can be built upon that, and that men and nations deviate from that at their peril.

For another thing, this nation under God requires *the discipline of a wider base of religious and moral education and training.* When all the smoke and fuming over the Supreme Court's decision about prayer in the schools have cleared away, we will still be left with two facts that yield neither to ecclesiastical controversy nor to court decisions:

1. Much that passes today in the name of religious education fails to contribute to a readiness to obey the laws of God or to the practice of decency in human relations.

2. There are about fifty million people in America today who do not attend church or synagogue, do not make any intelligent or devotional use of the Bible in their homes, and do not send the children outside the home for religious instruction. We had better take a long look at the wider base for religious and moral education and training in its application.

For a third thing, we need *the discipline of a clearer concept of our trusteeship.*

On a little island in the Western Pacific where some Americans and New Zealanders died, I found a rustic altar near the graves and it bore this inscription, "They shall not grow old as we who are left grow old. Age shall not weary them nor the years condemn. At the going down of the sun and in the morning we shall remember them."

It is well that we remember them. Soon the men who were the companions of the fallen, the eye witnesses, will pass from the scene, and the heroic sacrifices will pass from memory. There must be a teaching of history, a history that is linked with an interpretation of the price men had to pay to preserve our heritage, and it must not be divorced from the faith and devotion to country that inspired the sacrifices that were involved. Let it be a solemn warning that "the chosen people of the Lord" were reduced to a life of slavery when there arose in Egypt a ruler who knew not Joseph. We need to take a long look at our heritage, what it has cost, and at our trusteeship and the responsibilities it entails.

Finally, we need *the disciplines of courageous faith to move forward to embrace our destiny.* I am not speaking of the so-called manifest destiny about which Americans talked at the turn of the century, which assumed an automatic progress unrelated to our conduct and our character. Indeed, I suspect that what is basically wrong with our conduct is that dependable character is in short supply. I am speaking of our destiny *in terms of our responsibility and opportunity as they are related to the all-embracing purpose of the Lord of history.* It is the destiny envisioned in the prayer prayed by multiplied millions of his children, through sixty generations, "Thy kingdom come. Thy will be done on earth, as it is in heaven." While we rely upon the protection of divine Providence we must follow the Lord of history.

I cannot escape the conviction that this is the day of destiny for America. The day of destiny has come to others. Jesus stood one evening on the slope of Scopus and wept for his nations, saying, "Thou knewest not the time of thy visitation." I do not need to call the roll of the nations which in their hour of visitation repudiated God. It is only necessary to note that their candlesticks were removed and their opportunity passed.

This is our day of destiny. Never did any nation before us have such resources of power, such stores of plenty, such technical skills, or such reservoirs of compassion that can be tapped for human betterment. We shall embrace our destiny with valor, and walk with God. Or we shall fail, and failing sink back into the darkness that envelops the nations that forget God.

The Spiritual Basis for Peace

EDWARD H. PRUDEN

☆ ☆ ☆ As individuals we recognize our need of Almighty God. We make that recognition without apology and without embarrassment, for we have long since discovered that the great objectives of life become realities not through the exercise of our human efforts but by our willingness to accept these gifts from God alone who can make them possible.

This could be illustrated in numerous ways, but I should like to illustrate it in its relationship to the one great objective of mankind for peace in our time.

We discovered in 1918 and 1945 that this peace does not become our experience through the winning of great wars. In a long series of international conferences, we have discovered that peace does not become a reality through negotiations.

I was in the city of Paris on the twenty-seventh day of August in 1928 when the Kellogg-Briand Pact was signed—a pact which outlawed war as a means of settling international disputes. We felt that we were standing on holy ground as we waited outside the French Foreign Office while the great historic document came into being; but we were doomed to disappointment because we learned later, if we did not know it then, that peace is not of man's making. Peace is of the Spirit and must come to us as a result of our response to the influences of Almighty God.

This is not meant to cast any reflection on the United Nations or any other serious negotiations among nations; it is only meant to emphasize that the ultimate answer to the problems which perplex us must deal with man's inner nature—the source of our major difficulties.

We also discovered that peace does not become our possession by transferring our rightful, individual responsibilities for peace to the shoulders of officials whom we have appointed to places of leadership in the life of the nation. Our leaders can go no further morally and spiritually than we are prepared to go with them. And even if they should devise a perfect plan for peace, it would not work because we are an imperfect people. Someone has said that no possible rearrangement of bad eggs will make a good omelet, it is equally true that no possible rearrangement of men and maps, as they are, will result in peace; for there is something in the spirit of man which makes for misunderstanding and bloodshed and destruction. It is within the spirit of man that we must find the answer to the problem of war.

We live in a world remarkably like the world in which Jesus lived. Though the outward appearance of things has changed tremendously, underneath these exterior changes there are remarkable similarities. Jesus lived in an occupied country. When he walked the streets of Jerusalem, he saw the soldiers of Rome parading the thoroughfares. It was in the midst of this kind of situation that Nicodemus came with a question by night; and as they talked together, there must have passed between them some interesting and historic observations. We have a partial account of that encounter in the New Testament. I think that we shall not do violence to what happened, however, if we should use our imaginations a bit. I can imagine that Nicodemus said to Jesus: "Master, we are living in a hard, cruel, materialistic world. You have been telling us about justice, righteousness, love, human sympathy, understanding, and the kingdom of God. It is obvious, however, that we do not live in that kind of world. We live in a land which is overrun by a despised foe. We dare not speak our honest opinions. Our time-honored liberties have been taken from us. Now, Master, how can you ever reconcile the two? The realistic world of which we are a part and the spiritual world of which you are speaking?" And then it was that Jesus said: "Nicodemus, we shall never have this world of peace and brotherhood until individuals experience the transforming power of God in their hearts."

When I was teaching for a year in China before coming to live in Washington, I visited the Great Wall of China, which you know is considered one of the seven great wonders of the world. It was built at great cost of human life, money, effort, and time, for the purpose of keeping the enemy to the north from penetrating the Chinese territory to the south. It was so wide that two chariots could pass on top of the wall. It was made as strong as human ingenuity could make it; but I was told upon visiting the wall that in the first few years after its construction, the enemy penetrated the wall three times. Not by climbing over it, it was too well guarded. Not by breaking it down, it had been too well constructed. The enemy penetrated the wall simply by bribing the gate-keepers. In other words, the strength of the wall was actually no stronger than the character of the men who kept the gates.

We labor and pray for peace and brotherhood among the nations of the earth today; but down in our hearts, when we're perfectly honest with ourselves, we know that this does not come by the winning of wars, the holding of conferences, or by transferring our individual responsibilities for peace to the officials in conspicuous places. We know that peace is of the Spirit.

We had in our congregation for a while, in 1938, the Japanese Ambassador to the United States. When he came to Washington, I was alerted by a missionary friend of mine in Tokyo that he was a very devout Christian, a member of our communion, and that he was terribly disturbed over the deteriorating circumstances characterizing our relations with Japan, that he needed friendship and understanding, and would appreciate some attention.

We invited him to our church immediately, and later selected him to be the speaker at our annual dinner. I shall never forget how, in the course of his remarks, he reached into his pocket and pulled out a billfold on which had been attached a little gold plate and then explained that, when he was leaving Tokyo, several of his Christian friends held a dinner in his honor and gave him this present. On the little gold plate, they had ingraved the words from the New Testament "I am an ambassador for Jesus Christ." And then he said to us, "That is my supreme ambition. I would rather be that than anything else in the world."

It was not long thereafter that he was recalled to Japan and replaced by another who was here in the Japanese Embassy at the time of Pearl Harbor. I shall always believe that he was recalled partly because he could not conscientiously carry out his country's orders during those critical days.

I didn't see him during the days of the conflict, but he came back to Washington after the war was over, and we renewed our friendship. When I asked him what he was doing now, he said that he was helping to train young Japanese diplomats in the art of Christian democracy. Again and again, I have thought of that outstanding Japanese Christian and have been reminded that if prior to Pearl Harbor more of the Japanese people had shared his spirit and more of the American people had reflected the same spirit the conflict between the two countries would have been absolutely impossible.

We have tried numerous methods to establish peace and goodwill among the nations. We who are Christians know that the Master's plan for peace more than nineteen hundred years ago still is the only genuine assurance we have that peace will ever become a reality.

As Paul stated in his letter to the Ephesians, according to Goodspeed's translation, Christ has "broken down the barrier that kept us apart . . . [and] out of the two parties [has created] one new man by uniting them with himself." A religion with reservations is a religion that divides life into compartments, giving God complete authority over only a portion of one existence, but reserving other portions for one's own decisions. A religion *without* reservation is one which recognizes that without God we can do nothing but that with God all things are possible—even the establishment of peace in human hearts.

Facing New Frontiers

LATON E. HOLMGREN

☆☆☆ During prayers, I have found myself interceding for the success of the Christian message and mission throughout the world from Washington to Waikiki, from Tonga to Tokyo, from Bangkok to Beirut, and from Leopoldville to Lima.

But as I prayed I could not escape the disturbing question as to whether, in fact, the Christian faith was prevailing in today's world, whether on the frontiers of the world—not the geographical frontiers merely but the psychological, moral, and spiritual frontiers of earth— we are actually winning in the desperate struggle for the minds and souls of men.

The apparent answer to that question is that we are not. Despite the astronomical sums spent by our government, despite the further large amounts sent by private organizations and philanthropies and despite the vast expanse—and expense—of the Christian world mission, we seem to be losing ground.

The fact is that even after almost two thousand years of Christian history and evangelism there are today in the world more non-Christians than there were on the day of Pentecost. And so I should like to raise two questions: What are the reasons for this seeming decline of the things we hold most dear in the world? and What are some suggested remedies?

What are the reasons? There must be scores of them, but I will mention four only.

The first of these is the exploding populations of the earth which makes it almost impossible for us to keep up with the growth in the numbers of peoples of the world. The figures are staggering. Simply to say there is an increase in the population of the world every year of about forty million people does not somehow convey anything to us. But let me put it this way: Every thirty seconds, or about as long as it will take me to complete this sentence, eighty-five persons are born in the world; forty-five persons die during that same period; leaving a net increase in the world's population—every thirty seconds—of forty persons! The sobering fact is that accessions to the Christian faith do not even approximate those fantastic figures.

A second reason we confront is the advancing literacy and learning in the world. Probably one of the most revolutionary events in our world today is the amazing spread of literacy and education. It is estimated that at least twenty million adults learn to read and write for the first time each year. My own belief is that when future historians write the story of our age they will say far more about this being the era of literacy and learning than they will about its being the age of nuclear power.

The thing that is depressing about this is that men of questionable intent and sinister purpose are moving rapidly to win the uncommitted peoples of the world, particularly those who are now learning to read and write for the first time. They are using vast expenditures, able craftsmen, and determined methods to make their case, and in many places on earth are successfully winning the day.

A third reason for the lack of advance of the Christian faith is found in the rising revolutionary moods and movements of our day. We have all become so familiar with the cry of subjugated peoples that we hardly hear them anymore. Despite all we have tried to do to lift depressed humanity in recent years, there are more men and women on the verge of starvation today than there were fifty years ago. Will you imagine that you heard a knock on your front door just now and that when you opened it you saw standing in his tattered rags one of the emaciated, diseased men of the earth. As you were about to offer the poor fellow a piece of bread, you noticed that standing just behind him was another just like him. And behind him still another, and another. That line of hungry, distressed men and women at your front door this morning would reach around the world and return to your house, not once, but twenty-five times.

The fourth reason is the awakening ancient religions of the world. Everywhere we are seeing the revival of ancient faiths. Men are rebuilding their crumbled shrines, repairing their broken altars and even launching aggressive world missions. While we can only be grateful that men are everywhere trying to find the true God, we are dismayed to hear their preachers and prophets saying that the "East is spiritual; the West is secular." Christianity has been weighed in the balances and found wanting.

It has been the dominant world religion for nearly two thousand years and yet it has been unable to eradicate hatred and fear, to smother prejudice and bigotry, to banish cruelty and war. On the contrary, they are saying, the Christian nations have been the prime source of imperialism, the author of two world wars, and now they threaten to unleash such destructive power that none may survive its holocaust.

These are some of the reasons I believe there seems to be a decline in the Christian faith and Christian way of life. Let me suggest some remedies that come to mind this morning.

If we are to win in this struggle for the minds and souls of men, we must take to them a message that will be at once commanding and convincing.

In the first place, it must be clear enough for all to understand it. This obviously means that the message must be in a man's own language. One group of people we should give special thought to in our prayers is that army of men and women who today are translating the Christian message, either in the Scriptures or in Christian literature, into the languages of the world and adding fifteen or so new ones every year. It is quite impossible to describe the magnitude of this achievement. Probably no one can ever measure the privation involved, the depth of dedication, the hours of devoted study, the suffering and hardship endured to make these translations possible.

Let me try to illustrate it in this way. In trying to put the Bible into the Bambako language in West Africa, a great important tribe on the West Coast of Africa, the translator came up against the difficulty of translating the word "redemption." There was no such word in Bambako. But you cannot translate the New Testament without being able to say "redeemed" and "redemption" in some way. After working for weeks with his informants, who were native speakers of the language, one day one of them said: "We don't have a word for it, but we have an idiom —God took our heads out." The translator expressed curiosity and asked for an explanation. He was told that these peoples' forefathers were victims of the slave trade. When the young men were captured they were chained together by means of a collar placed around each victim's neck. A story was told that once one of the good tribal chiefs happened to see such a line of young men chained for slavery and in the group recognized the son of one of his favorite lieutenants—a man who had distinguished himself in tribal wars. He could not bear to see this young man sold into slavery and so negotiated for his release. When he finally met the price of release the chief went back to the line to the boy and "took his head out" of the collar. And the boy was redeemed. Today if you could read Bambako, you would find in the Bambako New Testament that whenever the word "redeemed" occurs in English, the Bambako idiom "God took our heads out" is used in its place.

Again, if we are to win in this global conflict, we must provide men with a message that is attractive enough for them all to want it. The Bible Society endeavors to publish the Scriptures in a form that will appeal to people, especially those who are unfamiliar with its contents. For most of us in America, the Bible is a sacred book, bound in somber black covers with royal gold edges. But to many people in the world these plain black covers are not attractive or appealing and may even be misleading. I was in the Congo not so long ago visiting the Kituba people in the Kasai Valley. The first New Testament in their language was on the press in the United States. The Christian Kituba were really excited about the prospect of having the whole New Testament in their own language for the first time. As I sat at lunch one day with some of the

African pastors, I showed them my English New Testament with its black covers and gold edges and asked if such a book would appeal to their tribal people. They looked at my book with uncertainty. Black, they said, was regarded by their people as the color of the devil. They said that were we to offer this book to a Kituba unbeliever, he would likely run for the bush in fright. The black covers would surely make this book seem to be some message from the devil. Instead they asked that we publish their Bible with bright yellow covers and today if you were to wander through the jungle of the Southern Congo you would see the Christians carrying their bright yellow New Testaments to church.

Furthermore, the message must be easy enough for all to reach it. Let us pray for all those who have gone out from this country all across the world to carry this message of the gospel of Jesus Christ to men and women everywhere. This Book has gone forth into every nation under heaven today because of the efforts of men and women who have been devoted to carrying the message of the gospel to the men of the earth.

Finally, if we are to win in this tremendous struggle, the message we take to men must be great enough so they all can be saved by it. Men everywhere are seeking answers to the distressing problems of our time. They are looking for a light that will lead to life. They are looking for a way that will lead to peace. That light and that way will be found only by accepting him who is revealed on the pages of the Bible.

This search for a way of salvation is characteristic of all the great faiths of the world. Too often we Christians fail to appreciate the important insights of the other great historic religions. Our own Scriptures tell us that God "did not leave himself without witness" (RSV). These other religions have produced great teachers who have told their people of the difference between the broad easy way that leads to death and the narrow difficult one that leads to life, and their people have tried to avoid the one and find the other. But despite their best efforts, they stand in the presence of good and evil and cry with the apostle Paul, "The good that I would I do not: and the evil which I would not, that I do. . . . Who shall deliver me?" It is only when a man meets Christ on the pages of this Book that he finds the Saviour he has been seeking. For Christ not only tells men the difference between good and evil, but, in their struggle to avoid the one and pursue the other, he takes them by the hand and says, "Let us walk this way together." Only when Christ enters their lives do men find the answers to life's most perplexing problems, its most distressing frustrations and its most terrifying fears. If we are to win in the struggle for the minds and souls of men, we must take them this message in more than a thousand tongues, so they may know the Saviour of the world, their Saviour and ours.

I close as I began: In the orbit of intercession for the success of the Christian mission from Washington to Waikiki, from Tonga to Tokyo, from Bangkok to Beirut, and from Leopoldville to Lima, let us pray that God's way and his will may be done in the world. Amen.

The Prospects for the United Nations

NORMAN COUSINS

☆☆☆ No single lesson in history was more urgent to the men who met in Philadelphia in 1787 than that peace is too important to be left to last-minute conferences. There was no place in their thinking for the notion that the most successful work in the world could be hastily improvised by political chieftains who had been riding hard all along in different directions. The genius of the Constitution makers was that they read themselves out of the picture. They fitted themselves into something larger and more durable than an *ad hoc* approach to survivial and freedom. That larger something was a Constitutional framework of law in which all men, including the heads of the states themselves, had specific obligations. And along with the obligations went firm limitations on the power of individuals.

The American federation makers placed their reliance not on the variable moods of men but on the rules of the game and the machinery that could make it work. Not that human agencies could be dispensed with; even laws had to be interpreted and enforced by men. But laws at least defined the standard and supplied the yardsticks of justice.

Without laws each man would be his own court and enforcement agency. This would incline him to conflict as naturally as he would start up at a strange sound in the dark. Law might not always work. It might be corrupted or distorted, but that only emphasized the need to restore it and bolster it and not to dispense with it.

Summit meetings can reduce tensions. They can result in mutual pledges to abstain from further development or manufacture of the continental pulverizing explosives. These pledges might even be backed up by agreements to make each nation accessible to inspectors from other nations. All this is helpful, but it doesn't meet the problem where the problem exists. The real problem is not agreement or treaty but law. It is the kind of law that operates under a sovereignty of its own in the area of world peace. It requires a specific structure of world organization which is not subordinate to the individual nations in matters of arms control or world security. It inspects and enforces not because it is permitted to do so but because that is its clearly defined job. It can use all the goodwill it can get, but it doesn't count on it, and it can exercise its authority without it if it has to.

The heads of states are not to be blamed if their crisis meetings skirt the real problem. For they are themselves prisoners of the very sovereignty they have come to protect and preserve. Thus meetings at the top level tend to be limited to a reshuffling of old factors rather than the creation of the necessary new ones.

It might be useful for men at the summit to consider why a summit meeting should be necessary in the first place. If the machinery of the United Nations had been able to do the job intended for it, there would be no need for top-level meetings. If the U.N. is to survive, what is necessary is not so much the willingness of the individual nations to refer matters to the U.N. but the built-in authority of the U.N. that can act whether the nations like it or not. At present, the U.N. acts when it has the consent of the parties involved. Thus it becomes an arbitration agency instead of a law-making and law-enforcing agency. Any policeman who is required to obtain the consent of a law-breaker before he, the policeman, can do his job is not a policeman but a supplicant. The men who lead the nations have the obligation to agree to a revision conference of the U.N. for the purpose of converting it from an arena of unlimited options to an organization of binding obligations.

Such a revision conference might in fact and in truth justify the use of the term "summit meeting." Its job will be to tame the nations, to define the principles of justice in the world, to bring under rigid control the nuclear arsenals, and to create the basis for the responsible administration of the affairs of the human community.

Even when we do all this, there is no guarantee that it will work. But it at least puts the resources of human intelligence and energy to work where they are most needed.

In order that binding commitments instead of tentative agreements be reached it may be essential to look beyond the emergency meetings to a full-scale convention of the nations. The agenda for such a convention would be swept clean of the usual items involving national prestige and power, thrust and counterthrust, plot and counterplot. There would be one major item on the agenda: the creation of a common authority with sovereignty of its own, responsible to the world's peoples, with enforceable powers over disarmament. In short, the agenda is survival.

If such powers existed in the United Nations today it would be neither necessary nor possible to summon a conference outside of it for the purpose of dealing with immediate threats to the peace. In fact, nothing more sharply dramatizes the nature of the present world anarchy than the fact that the U.N. is hardly even mentioned in the efforts to deal with such crises as Suez or Berlin.

No objection to the argument for enforceable world law is weaker than the one which says: "Sure, but how?" Adequate action begins with a declaration of intent. It advances through advocacy. It comes to life through special effort with some measure of dedication behind it. When this is done, we will be in a position to estimate either the difficulties or the possibilities or both but not before.

In our time it is not enough to convene the peak personalities. It becomes necessary to convene the peak ideas. Peace today is not to be found just by making a trip to some magic mountain but in putting tall thoughts and purposes to work. The credentials of the participants must be represented not by their titles or ribbons but by their ability to create a totally new way of life among the nations.

It would be foolish to expect any single plan for a restructured United Nations to produce a panacea for global problems. But at least a beginning can be made in eliminating such basic weaknesses of the United Nations as may now be complicating world tensions. Structurally one of the dangers of weak international organization is that it cannot provide adequate security for the individual nation, large or small. There is no real deterrent to aggression. Dynamic nations are tempted to exploit military vacuums wherever they can find them. Peace-loving nations are forced into elaborate armaments and defense preparedness. It is only a matter of time before there is a scramble for power and a saturation of tensions.

The United Nations Charter anticipates the need for change in its own structure. It provides for a general review conference for the purpose of considering basic new facts that may affect the future of the U.N.

How would a revision conference go about acting on new facts? What are the general problems that would probably come before a review conference of the United Nations?

Fundamentally, of course, the basic purpose of a review conference would be to explore the means by which the United Nations could enact, enforce, and interpret the rule of law. Moreover such a conference could offer the world a chance to wipe the slate clean. The benefits of participation in such a strengthened body should be equally available to all. Membership should be universal. Any nation sincerely interested in security and the common welfare of the world's peoples should have no hesitation in joining with the rest.

There are benefits, but there are also obligations and responsibilities. The durable, meaningful peace to which humanity is entitled cannot be obtained without sacrifice.

The conditions for membership can be clearly stated: respect for the rules of the game, respect for the rights of the individual members, prompt fulfillment of obligations, recognition that the human community has precedence over the national community in those specific matters related to a common world security.

The United Nations is not a country club or a fraternal order. It should exist for the purpose of defining the obligations of nations and enforcing them. The more recalcitrant a nation, the more of a problem it represents to world order, the greater the need to have it within the jurisdiction of an ordered world. But universal membership in a U.N. also presupposes responsible authority on those matters affecting the peace.

The aim of a revised U.N., then, would be to have its own actual and potential forces, large enough to prevent aggression or to cope with it instantly if it should occur. As said earlier, it should be able to legislate effectively in the matter of national armaments; which is to say, the world's peoples must have confidence in the disarmament arrangements. It should enjoy the right of inspection to guard against secret manufacture of weapons adapted to mass destruction.

What sovereign rights ought the nations to retain? The individual nations have a right to insist on recapturing sovereignty over their own institutions and cultures. I use the word "recapturing" because sovereignty in domestic matters has been seriously weakened under world anarchy, with war or the fear of war determining the careers and destinies of millions of citizens, the size of their taxes, or the pressures upon free institutions.

Because of the sheer weight and complexity of all these questions, there is a real danger that a review conference could fall apart almost at the start. That is why it is so important, before any specific matters of substance are discussed, that the conference recognize frankly its own inability to come up with definitive answers at a *single* session. There should be an orderly and progressive consideration of the problems without any time limit as to expiration date of the meetings. For the conference must be more than another international meeting: It should be a congress of history and hope, studying man's efforts to govern himself in units of increasing size and complexity. It requires the most painstaking scrutiny of the historical record; it must combine wisdom with knowledge, insight with information, vision with comprehension. Three or four years or more is not too long a time for such a service to the world community. The Philadelphia Convention of the American states took the better part of two years, and the public debate continued for years more.

In particular, in organizing its work over the long range, the conference could divide itself into various parts. The initial full session of the conference could be concerned with a general discussion of problems and objectives. After the preliminary meetings, the group could be narrowed down to a working committee, with every nation having at least a single representative. The group would meet regularly with no fixed date for concluding its labors. At least twice a year, the full review conference could be reconvened for the purpose of receiving an interim report of the working committee and for advising the committee on the general pattern of its work.

The most difficult, yet most important, achievement of a working committee would no doubt be to suggest how the United Nations can have interim police powers until such time as the United Nations is invested with the general powers of world law. This may require a timetable for the execution of a four-phase plan for interim world security.

In the first phase of this timetable, the United Nations could be given command of modest military forces. This might come to approximately one million men under arms—a small figure as modern armies go but enough to serve symbolic purposes as well as to act as a deterrent for the type of aggression that, as in Korea, would try to capitalize on weak spots which might otherwise seem attainable at low cost. The U.N. army should be completely up-to-date. It should have access to such weapons as would be required to cope with the arsenal of any possible law-breaker.

The precedent for the establishment of such a force is Korea itself, with two significant differences. One is that the U.N. would have to wait until the aggression was actually committed before recruiting a force of its own. The force would now be preventive rather than combative in purpose. The second difference is that the U.N. would no longer have to rely on the nation most vitally concerned to furnish the bulk of men and material. Surely the common cause of an enforceable peace is compelling enough for a fair and mandatory sharing of obligations. No question of good or bad faith is involved. Rather there must be a complete understanding by all nations concerning their world obligations and fixed responsibilities. No nation should have a valid basis for complaining that its own contribution is out of proportion to the total effort.

In the second phase of the timetable for interim security, the plan for enforceable disarmament could come up. On the assumption that the U.N. force would have served its purpose—namely, to act as a shield behind which the U.N. could develop a sound basis for a workable peace —the next step would be control over national armaments. A bona fide request should be made of *all* nations. In return for participation in the plan for enforceable disarmament, each nation would have its security underwritten by the U.N., which by now would have substantial military authority, plus a call on immediate additional strength as needed.

The appeal of this proposal lies in the fact that the question of disarmament could now be considered inside an entirely different framework from the one that history had discredited. The new framework should have nothing to do with treaties or conventions—history is littered with the wreckage of such treaties and conventions. The new framework should be concerned with workable machinery, with enforcement measures, in short, with disarmament under law. No talk of disarmament makes sense, no proposed quotas for reduction of armaments is possible unless the world's peoples could be confident that the success of any plan rests on something firmer than the good intentions of the agreeing parties.

In particular, a workable disarmament plan should call for control of all weapons adapted to mass destruction. Inspections and sanctions are mandatory to keep nations from engaging in such manufacture. Atomic energy, for example, should be developed under proper safeguards, with each nation participating as its own resources and industrial establishments would permit and deriving benefits in proportion to the individual contribution to the overall effort. This would not exclude other states from atomic benefits, particularly where health and economic development are concerned, but it would leave to those states with atomic-energy installations the primary rights of development and use for peaceful purposes. The U.N. inspectors would maintain careful safeguards against diversion of such facilities for military purposes. The U.N. would cease to manufacture atomic weapons once universal membership is achieved in the U.N. and the means for preventing war established.

The principal difference between this plan for control of atomic armaments and earlier proposals is that the U.N. would now be given powers against war itself. Under the Baruch Plan, for example, atomic disarmament was sought without any comparable machinery for dealing with the circumstances which might dictate the use of atomic weapons. No state under the proposed plan could justifiably argue that control of atomic energy was now being pursued in a vacuum, or that there was no agency strong enough to protect it against war and to ensure its rights.

The third phase of the work of the review conference might grow out of the previous two. Just as investing the U.N. with appropriate forces of its own is the precondition for any plan for enforceable disarmament, so the need to create a durable structure for carrying out disarmament would raise the question: What about the overall form of the U.N. itself?

This form is inevitably related to its own powers and limitations. Law begins with the conquest of force. It moves through the agencies of justice and enforcement. It never allows potential violators to become stronger than the machinery to deal with violators. It is in the implementation of this idea that government takes shape. Whether that government is good or bad, whether it is a government in which all men are subject to the laws, including the leaders, or whether it is a government in which the laws serve the purposes of a few men or a man bent on capturing the state and its people—all these questions depend upon the wisdom and courage of the founders, the popular mandate behind them, and their ability to retain the confidence of the world's peoples.

It seems inescapable that the principles of federalism would have to be seriously examined by a review conference if the United Nations is to possess adequate authority in the area of common security yet also be able to guarantee retention of internal sovereignty to the individual nations. Let us consider the alternatives.

First, a league. A league is a loose organization of states held together by treaty with the individual nations retaining ultimate authority even in armaments or other matters related to the common security. In view of the failures of leagues throughout history, including the United Nations and the League of Nations itself, it is to be hoped that the delegates would not tempt history further.

Second, a confederation. A confederation is a step beyond a league; that is to say, an attempt is made at a fairly organic relationship among the states and the obligations of all nations are generally fairly well defined. What a confederation lacks, however, is a structural basis for exacting obligations or for the adequate enforcement of its own rules. It lacks a common authority transcending national authority in those matters clearly concerned with common dangers and common needs.

Third, a strong central government. It is doubtful that the historic conditions exist at the moment for a strong central government of the world. Indeed the easiest way to kill a centralized United Nations is to impose upon it functions and powers far beyond its capacity. A central government taking upon itself all the powers exercised by the individual nations—powers in the fields of taxation, currency, immigration, trade, economic development, mutual security and defense, general welfare, and so forth—would be dealing with such complexities and imponderables as could bring about its possible early collapse. Moreover, the differences in national institutions and cultures might create an almost insurmountable barrier for any government which attempted to maintain jurisdiction over the individual.

This leaves what is probably the soundest and safest approach of all to the revised structure of the U.N.; namely, a federation of limited but adequate powers. In such a federation, each nation would retain jurisdiction over its people and institutions in all matters except those clearly related to the common security and common development. There would be clear-cut distinctions between world jurisdiction and national jurisdiction, between the sovereignty that would be pooled in the federation and the sovereignty retained by the national states. The powers of a federated U.N. would be specifically confined to common needs and common dangers.

So far as jurisdiction over the individual is concerned, it would be restricted to those matters affecting the security of all peoples. The Nuremberg trials, it will be recalled, proceeded on the principle of individual responsibility and guilt for acts leading to war. What is needed now is exactly the same principle, except that this time the guilty parties should be apprehended in time to avert war rather than after the damage has been done and the dead counted.

Economic development, especially in the case of Asia and Africa, should be a signal opportunity for the federated U.N. It should be recognized, however, that many of the nations of Asia and Africa are just extricating themselves from a century or more of outside rule and that nothing should be done which could be regarded by those states as interference with their problems of internal development and control. Hence it should be made clear that any requests for economic, technological, or scientific assistance to individual nations are to originate from the nations themselves. The greatest care should be taken to see that each development project would operate in a way consistent with each nation's own culture and institutions and that its own facilities with human resources would be fully utilized.

The U.N. already has within it many excellent agencies in the fields of world health, food, refugee problems, education, science, and so forth. But two things are in the way of their effective operation. The first is that these groups lack any real authority or the means of carrying out the necessary programs. The second is that the dominant energies and resources of most of the nations are being diverted to military purposes. The combination of authority and means could enable the special agencies of the U.N. to demonstrate high usefulness in improving the conditions of human existence.

These agencies, of course, would be directly responsible to and established by the legislative branch of the U.N.

Where would all this authority be lodged? In the General Assembly? The Security Council? It is doubtful that the big states would like to see important powers given to the General Assembly in its present form in view of the fact that they are on even footing with states with only a fraction of their own populations. Meanwhile, the Security Council, run by the big states, is bound by the unanimity principle. This means that no issue of consequence involving the major nations can be settled at present on the basis of strict adherence to law, for a major nation could negate the law through the veto.

Any attempt to redefine the authority of the General Assembly and Security Council, however, squarely opens up the entire question both of representation and of division of powers.

If a purely democratic basis were used for representation, then two or three populous nations might be able to dominate the voting. If a one-vote-for-one-state basis were used, then a few small states with perhaps an aggregate population of twenty million might be able to outvote nations with an aggregate population of 750,000,000 or more. This is perhaps the thorniest problem of all. There can be no authority without representation, but representation under existing circumstances seems impossible.

This dilemma may yield to the concept of *dual federalism* based on a regional approach inside the United Nations. Under this arrangement the General Assembly could be divided into its component regional parts, each of which would receive a total of one hundred votes or less, depending upon population, size, resources, and other vital factors. Each region would determine for itself the voting procedures for its own members in arriving at decisions concerning the vote that would be cast by the unit as a whole. A regional unit consisting of, say, ten members, two of which had a combined population larger than the combined total of the remaining eight members, might wish to give proportionate weight to the larger members in working out an equitable system of representation within itself. A regional unit might wish to split its hundred votes in the General Assembly in order to reflect the mixed voting within itself on any question.

The advantage of the regional arrangement goes far beyond the possible solution it offers to the impasse of representation by population as against representation by nation. It recognizes a certain grouping of interests on the regional level—economic, cultural, political—and provides the means by which these natural interests could be protected and advanced.

The only questions on which the regional units need be called upon to vote as units in the General Assembly would be on matters involving the common security or on relations of units to one another or on the relations of members of one unit to members of another.

Dual federalism, then, is federalism of nations within regional units and federalism of nations as members of regional units on the world level. The nation, the regional unit, and the federated U.N. would each exercise such sovereignty as was natural to it. The individual nations would have authority and jurisdiction in all matters pertaining to their own institutions and internal affairs. The regional units would have authority and jurisdiction in all matters pertaining to the regional needs and interests of its members. Finally, a federated U.N. would have authority and jurisdiction in those matters directly affecting the safety and vital needs of the world community.

As part of this general proposal, the Security Council might have to be reconstituted as an Executive Council. Its primary function would be to carry out the wishes and enforce the decisions of the General Assembly. The Executive Council would elect its own chairman and vice chairman, subject to ratification by the General Assembly. All the special agencies—disarmament, atomic controls, world health, food, economic development, refugees, and so forth—of the U.N. would come within the administration of the council. The operating budget of the council and its agencies would have to come before the General Assembly, which would have powers of appropriation and review.

The Executive Council, unlike its predecessor, the Security Council, would not be concerned with votes or vetoes within itself. It would not be a legislative agency but the principal enforcement arm of the United Nations. As such, it could make recommendations but it could not enact legislation or review it.

Judicial review of legislation enacted by the General Assembly and of the enforcement activities of the Executive Council would be vested in a World Court.

Historically the basic energy of this country has come from great ideas. I believe the United States will discover its greatest strength when it provides leadership in the world for the idea that nations themselves must submit to a rule of law.

What we seek—not just for ourselves, but for all men—is justice, and justice is possible only under law. I would hope, therefore, that the American people would put their support of the United Nations to work in the making of a better and stronger United Nations.

The United Nations cannot solve all the world's problems. But it may release resources to man for higher ends—the pursuit of justice and a purposeful life. And if nothing else is achieved, at least for the first time in history the human community would have its own voice.

If We Fulfill the World's Hope

BROOKS HAYS

⭐⭐☆ If I were required to have a text I think it would be the words of our beloved President. He said sometime ago that if we fulfill the world's hope, it will be by fulfilling our own faith. What kind of faith do we have? We have an individualistic faith. We know that the commitment of the individual is the life cell of a Christian society. We believe with the great theologian who said that "it is only religion reaching the ultimate solitude of the soul that can create the unpurchasable man." It is only the man of integrity and man unpurchasable by any society that can create the sound society. So as we rededicate ourselves in faith to our Christian tradition, which is our most precious value in American life, we are aware above everything else that our faith is individual, that in the heart and soul of one man are focused all of the final values of human existence.

I think of the comfort of religion that comes to individual men and women, because one time as a lonesome lad in Camp Pike, during the brief experience of mine as a soldier, I was disconsolate, I was not well physically, and in that attitude of despondency, I went to the service—a Protestant service in the YMCA hut long before the government had charted these plans for commodious chapels. But there was a chaplain bringing me a message of the Bible. Our faith is biblical, and because it is biblical, it had this beginning in concern for the individual. And this chaplain didn't know that he was preaching to someone who needed very much the text that he used. These were his words. The words from Job. "[The Lord] knoweth the way that I take: when he hath tried me, I shall come forth as gold." I wish I could find that chaplain to tell him that for four decades and more I have recalled those words and some of the spirit of that consoling message, which religion alone can give and supply to one who needs it.

But I have an idea that none of us will ever have the greatest need of faith and consolation and solace of religion. I think Helen Keller could speak more authoritatively than anyone, and I like to recall her words because in her life the strength of faith was available and was tested. She made the statement that "one would have to live in a dark and silent world to understand fully the precious comfort of religion." I think that, of all professions, the soldier, the sailor, the members of our military services can speak authoritatively about the strength that comes from religion, particularly during the period of their lives when there is danger surrounding them. And it bears out my point that our national faith begins with this concern for the individual and a faith that God's care constantly surrounds us.

I remember the words of the Australian airman, Sergeant Hugh Brodie.

> Almighty and all present Power,
> Short is the prayer I make to Thee,
> I do not ask in battle hour
> For any shield to cover me.
>
> The vast unalterable way,
> From which the stars do not depart
> May not be turned aside to stay
> The bullet flying to my heart.
> .   .   .   .
> But this I pray, be at my side
> When death is drawing through the sky,
> Almighty God who also died
> Teach me the way that I should die.

It is Christian faith that supplies for our men in arms the influences that sustain them in every danger.

Now there is reserved a day—not on November 11, when there was a triumph of arms that will be celebrated always in America, but Memorial Day—to pay tribute to those who did not return. Yet it is inevitable that on November 11 a grateful people would be thinking of the men who made the supreme sacrifice in the great wars that followed our tragic civil war of the nineteenth century. And I believe that when President Kennedy used the expression, "fulfilling the world's hope," he was conveying into the twentieth century the eloquent words of President Lincoln who referred to America as "the last best hope of earth." As we exalt a faith that is biblical, we are exalting a faith that may have a national expression, for our lives are so bound up together that when dangers surround us we feel a sense of unity that an awareness of God's mercy supplies. We are his children. We know how to evaluate religion; we know how to fit it to our constitutional doctrines. And the distinguished doctrine of separation of church and state cannot be construed to imply that religion and government are not related. The wall of separation that was spoken of by a very devout man, Thomas Jefferson, was regarded as an impregnable wall to separate these two areas of life, but it was not an impenetrable wall, for there are openings in it so that those in government may have access to the resources of faith.

I say this as a layman in acknowledgment of my appreciation of what is done week after week in services of this kind to the end that military and governmental policies may be rooted in the life of faith. We do not believe that America fights holy wars—we have no thought of using our unprecedented and incomparable industrial and military power for aggression to dominate other nations. We believe that we have fought just wars and there is a distinction. We have fought just wars, and justice must have implementation. So there is a feeling that the great strength of our military armaments, the new and ingenious weaponry that we have constructed is quite consistent with our desire for peace and the spiritual goals in our distraught world. I think it is appropriate for us to speak of this individualistic and biblical faith as also a corporate faith and to have a sense of national mission that becomes a people who have benefited so greatly from our Christian religion. Our faith in that sense is universal, since it is national. One raises the question of whether it can be universal. Indeed it is, and America has no objectives in the world, no goals to pursue that are not compatible with our love of our fellow human beings where-ever they live under whatever flag they exist.

I remember that Dan Poling was himself a distinguished chaplain in the first world war. He told me of an experience of his when one of the soldiers came to him at the height of fighting in France—he was a sniper—and said, "Padre, awhile ago I saw a Dutchman, and in a moment I did not see him." And then Dan Poling told that this big strong American lad said (fighting back the tears), "I hope to God he doesn't have a wife and baby at home like I have." And Dan and I agreed that there came into that conversation in that simple reference the element of compassion that we want to glorify in the American armed services.

A Methodist minister came into my office one day when I served in Congress and identified himself as Dr. Tanny Moto, pastor of a Methodist Church in Iwo Jima. He said, "Mr. Hays, there is no bitterness in our hearts. We have conquered all of that. We want the American people to know we love them." And I think he was speaking sincerely, for there had been every evidence that our messages of goodwill made it easy for them to respond in that fashion. May America always be true to this idea of Christain love and compassion, for it does bring returns that we could classify as selfish and in our national interest, though the motiva-tions are surely higher than that.

But I think this analysis of faith would be incomplete by simply saying that it is individual, it is biblical, it is corporate, and finally that it is universal and embraces all men and all nations.

So I would like to include the other stanza of that little poem by the pilot who served with the Australians in the second world war, It is, I think, a bit of literature that will survive.

> I ask no help to strike my foe,
> I ask no petty victory here,
> The enemy I hate, I know,
> To Thee is also dear.

Here is a triumph of faith, here is the crashing through of a good and devoted Christian to that high and exalted attitude of love and goodwill that was possible only because he believed that God is the Father of all men.

Therefore, it seems to me appropriate for us on Veterans' Day, the day that is so notable in our history, that means so much to us as Americans, to reconsecrate ourselves to the spiritual and religious bases for our greatness. For, as we have said, "If we fulfill the world's hope, it will be by fulfilling our own faith."

Thanksgiving in the American Way

EDWARD L. R. ELSON

☆ ☆ ☆ As Paul in his message to the early Christians at Thessalonica exhorted them to "stand firm and hold to the traditions which you were taught" (II Thess. 2:15, RSV), so we have foregathered to keep the tradition of our founding fathers. We do not come here to fondle a dead past nor to caress a forgotten antiquity. This event is not a relic from the museum but a living reality in life today. The day witnesses to the fact that we are a God-conscious people and that our life and destiny are under his sovereignty.

To the American people the most important thing about Thanksgiving Day is that we have it. It is one of the actions by which we testify that we are uniquely "a nation under God." The day heralds to the peoples of the world that the collective entity known as the United States of America is erected upon a theistic basis.

Thanksgiving Day is predicated upon the fact that as a nation we believe there is SOMEONE—someone spelled in capital letters—who is to be thanked. Only a nation with faith in the transcendent God over all of life, sovereign over individual man and over nations, can keep such a day.

The day derives its meaning from the fact we give primacy to God as the source of both individual and national existence.

This day begins with and derives its siginficance from the first words of the Bible, "In the beginning God . . ." Thanksgiving Day represents the explicit comingling of religion and government, of church and state. It is not an alliance of the institution of church with the institution of government, but it emphasizes the pervasiveness of religion in the whole of life. Congress has made a law establishing this day as a national religious day. And consonant with congressional action, the President of the United States sets it apart by proclamation, inviting the people to give thanks to Almighty God for his abundant blessings. The day testifies clearly to the infusion of religion in national life.

This is as it should be. It is derived from our heritage and is consistent with the basic thesis upon which our life has been developed. Apart from faith in God, American life has no meaning. Our ideals are religious ideals, our standards religious standards, our goals religious goals, our motivations, when we are truly ourselves, are religious motivations. This day then is more than a holiday; it is a holy day proclaiming a way of life. America has become great and strong not simply because of great natural resources, secured behind wide ocean frontiers and friendly neighbors. Rather, America has become great and strong because of a creative spirit derived from our religious faith mediated to American life by a variety of religious denominations. In some individuals this faith has been intimate and personal; in others it has been simply a way of life derived from the social climate and the cultural atmosphere produced by religious faith. You may not go to church every Sunday; you may even neglect your own prayers; but you are inheriting a way of life produced by those who do believe in God, who do go to church, who say their prayers, who do maintain a religious home and keep the spiritual disciplines of life.

First of all, we thank God we have a day of thanksgiving symbolic of the traditions we have been taught.

In the second place, we have genuine reasons for being thankful. Much evidence points to the fact that among the nations in the world in all human history we are at this time the most affluent. To look at current sales records and the flow of consumer goods we are made aware of the outpouring of God's bounty. Based upon current attitudes, individual

Americans today seem to have two chief concerns. An American asks first, "How can I reduce?" and second, "Where can I park my car?" Is not this a strange but interesting commentary in a world where millions of people are inadequately fed and where most people walk instead of ride?

Yet today, standing in the presence of Almighty God, we come to acknowledge that what we have is not an attainment but an obtainment. All that we have is a gift of God in response to creative and industrious labor. Moreover Thanksgiving Day is not dependent upon material prosperity. It is rather a way of believing and acting. As a people we have kept the day through periods of adversity as well as in days of great prosperity. It has been kept in times of war as well as in times of peace. At least nine times Thanksgiving Day was observed before the War for Independence. It was commemorated eight times during the long and terrible course of the war when the ragged, hard-pressed Colonial troops paused to thank God for their pitiful victories. Thanksgiving is not for mere abundance but to praise God for our survival as free men.

Has it ever occurred to you that no American has ever been more underprivileged than those who started this custom of setting aside a day of thanksgiving? They had no homes and no housing administration to help them build a home. Their only transportation was by foot. The clothing they had was inadequate, and had been brought with them on the Mayflower. Their only food came from the sea and the forest, and they had to get it for themselves. They had no money and no place to spend it if they had it. They had no amusements except those which they made for themselves, no neighbors but savages, no means of communicating with their relatives at home. But if anyone had called them underprivileged, he would in all probability have ended in the stocks. For they did have possessions that are among the greatest of human assets—initiative, courage, a willingness to work, and a boundless faith in God. In coming to the new land they had committed their cause to God, but they had not supinely reclined upon the notion that divine law was on their side regardless of whether they obeyed it or not. They understood to the full that men have obligations as well as rights.

Because our spiritual kinsmen, our pioneer forebears had initiative, courage, a will to work, and a religious faith, they survived, planted crops, reaped a harvest, and declared a thanksgiving. Their turkey came neither from a raffle ticket nor from a relief board. Nor were they too tired to go to church, although they had to shoulder muskets to ward off possible attacks of unfriendly people. Above all else, they believed in the depth of their being that political freedom was the logical culmination of spiritual emancipation and that individual man, standing in the majesty of his createdness and under the redemption wrought by Jesus Christ, was the kind of man who could be trusted with his own life and with his own destiny. It was a way of life derived from religious faith which they proclaimed and lived daily and which we have come here to renew.

It is easy for superficial men, unaware of the deeper meanings and hidden values in American culture, to say that the material progress we have experienced has debased spiritual values. In contrast to other societies, the fruits of material progress in the United States have provided the leisure, the energy, and the means for a level of human and spiritual values never before attained.

Sometimes foreigners see us better than we see ourselves. Peregrine Worsthorne, writing in the *London Daily Telegraph* and *Morning Post* about a recent visit to the United States, said:

Traveling from coast to coast and talking to innumerable Americans, both exalted and humble, I formed my own conclusions.

Here, it seemed to me, was a society in which men and women, families and communities, are realizing the good life not in the past or the future, not in slogans nor statistics, not in terms of ideology or propaganda, but actually on the grounds, in their flesh and blood lives, here and now . . .

So far as my eyes could see, so far indeed as any normal yardstick can measure, America today fulfills more of the criteria of a civilized society than any in human history. I make no apology for this panegyric. If the reader is as mislead about the current state of America as I was . . . until seeing for myself . . . then nothing short of this emphatic remonstrance can be enough to redress the balance.[1]

When we see what really has been happening here, as in all honesty others see us, we must not stop to boast but only to thank God and to pray that he will keep alive within us the profound truths and the ready disciplines which have made us what we are.

[1] Used by permission.

Today, as we remember God's goodness and mercy, his tenderness and generosity, let us give back in service to him the land he has given to us with a people renewed in spirit and dedicated to the fulfillment of that higher kingdom where love is law and God is supremely King. In much of the world today, that which has produced our way of life not only is rejected but ruthlessly opposed. In much of our world we see at work a vast imperialistic system of person-control, thought-control, property-control, which is precisely the opposite of the tradition Paul asked us to keep and which was espoused by Jefferson, Washington, Lincoln, Eisenhower, and other great patriots. "The God who made us, made us free," said Jefferson. But now the Communist says, "I will give you bread here and now but you must give the Socialist state your mind, your body, and your spirit." Where that system prevails, men and women have less, both of bread and freedom. Let us not be discouraged in the ideological conflict. We have great tactical advantages and tremendous resources, for when men are free, they transmit to others this infectious spirit of freedom under a sovereign God.

In a recent trip through seventeen countries our genius and strength and the Communist's defects and weaknesses have become crystal clear. In contrast to that order where men are herded from place to place, coerced, repressssed, and possessed, there is the free man with his outgoing friendliness, his distinctive goodwill, his overflowing energy. To be a free man under the sovereignty of the transcendent God is sufficient cause for celebrating Thanksgiving Day.

Let us now thank God and take courage not because we are God's pets but because we are his children and he is our Father—because what we are we owe to him. What we shall become we shall become by his wisdom and grace.

> Our father's God, to Thee,
> Author of liberty,
>   To Thee we sing:
> Long may our land be bright
> With freedom's holy light;
> Protect us by Thy might,
>   Great God, our King.

The Year Time Ran Out

GEORGE R. DAVIS

☆☆☆ I have chosen this title not because I wish to appear to be unusual or sensational but because it represents an actual fact. In a sense time did run out this year, indeed quite recently, at least psychologically speaking. For the first time the nation as a whole, or at least large segments of the nation, may see fairly clearly the meaning of the threat we confront, a threat to the world's survival. We should have seen this long ago. Some did. But of course we should have been able in another time to see the meaning of Adolph Hitler. This we did not see even when he documented his purpose in a rather brutal book. Present threats have also been documented in word and deed across decades. Perhaps it took Cuba to awaken us. Still hard to comprehend is the manner in which this came about on our very doorstep. But when we looked "down the atomic gun barrels," Russian provided and Russian manned, ninety miles off our shores, there is no question a large percentage of our population sensed for the first time the meaning of "the end of the world." The amazing support of our world neighbors in that crisis will remain a source of inspiration, and the disciplined spirit and calm of our own people generally, pointed up a cause for just pride. Even if we were to waste by carelessness that reservoir of international goodwill gained in a crisis, one could never forget it.

But time has run out. It actually ran out twenty years ago under a stadium at the University of Chicago. Enrico Fermi, climaxing long studies and secret experimentation, directed the pushing of a button, and a new age was born, an age which set in motion the possibility of atomic suicide for man. When later reporting the event, Dr. Fermi declared his uncertainty about what would happen when the button was pressed; it might have signaled the destruction of the stadium, the university, or the city of Chicago itself. That moment time ran out, and we were not wise enough to know it. Even the tragedies of Hiroshima and Nagasaki, and the warnings of philosophers, scientists, and not a few ministers across twenty years did not fully awaken us to that fact.

Even if we were to destroy all instruments of warfare, even though we achieve complete disarmament, worldwide and well policed, we must live from now on with the knowledge that man has the capacity to recreate them, the intellectual know-how to liquidate this planet. And it is in this sense time has run out. Let me repeat, it actually ran out twenty years ago. The realization has just caught up with us. We cannot go back now to the innocency of our pre-atom Garden of Eden.

I am hopeful about mankind, and by no means have surrendered to pessimism. I think we have really tried to give support to all the agencies of peaceful solution. I think we shall continue to do so. I do not find it possible to believe we shall as a nation throw caution to the winds, nor follow the lead of any irresponsible voices who tempt us to turn away from our dedication to sanity and our desire to help lead the world to permanent peace. And let us move forward with the certain knowledge that to fail now at this high task would be failure with a far higher price to pay, a final price, than would have been the case before time ran out, when we lived in a different age.

In the light of these facts can one be thankful now? I will not indulge in an expression of my own personal thanks for countless blessings which may not be the lot of all. But I will ask and then try to answer these questions: In the act of performing this formal ritual of thanksgiving today, a long tradition in our national life, are we on solid ground in so doing? Is this more than a diminishing rite in the year time ran out? May men be rationally thankful now? Does this day stand up under close scrutiny?

May I try to express for you our national thanksgiving, without being presumptuous? I am grateful first of all for the human struggle in history. It has been a long struggle up out of the darkness, and at times back into the darkness and out again. The struggle has had glorious moments on this continent too, from the beginning. I may not know how the struggle came to be born, or how it will end exactly. I have my notions and my faith. There are those who think the human struggle came out of the "mud and muck" and nothing more. I believe otherwise. But regardless of the origins, the human race has heroicly struggled, and some of the finest chapters were written on this continent, at Plymouth Rock, Valley Forge, Gettysburg but also in laboratories, universities, hospitals, councils of industry and labor. Who could count the places, marking the struggle of man in all times, and in all ages, on this planet? And I am grateful for this on our national Thanksgiving Day. And even if the long struggle were finally to end up on a dead-end street, which I most surely do not believe, I am grateful and proud of mankind's painful, persistent march. Human heroism, as suggested in these lines:

> A picket frozen on duty,
>   A mother starved for her brood,
> Socrates drinking the hemlock,
>   And Jesus on the rood;
> And millions who, humble and nameless,
>   The straight, hard pathway trod,—
> Some call it Consecration,
>   And others call it God.[1]

makes me proud and thankful. On our national day of thanksgiving let us be glad the human struggle has been made. There is a controversial play of our time which has in it at least one line worth remembering, uttered by a character expressing one of his feelings in a desperate age, "In the bloodiest of times, some remain human." Thank God for man's true humanity, and his relentless struggle. How grateful we should be for this thrilling adventure.

[1] "Each in His Own Tongue" by William Herbert Carruth.

Let us likewise be grateful today that there has been, and still is "by the grace of God," a place called the United States of America. Never in all of my life have I wanted to state this with more force. Like too many others, I have been hesitant to express it, fearful I would be arrogant and guilty of a kind of nationalism one does not care to possess or trust. I have spent the last few days in an institute dealing with national well-being as related to the common problems of Jews, Roman Catholics, and Protestants, indeed of all of our citizens. Out of this experience was born afresh in me something we too often forget or take for granted, which is this simple fact: There is no other place in all the world where hope is held out to such a degree for all groups, all races, all faiths. I dare to say this in spite of some evidences to the contrary. There are "dirty spots on our national linen," but there is no other place in all the world where the dirty linen is put up to dry so openly before the whole world. Indeed we have tended to hang out the dirty linen with regularity, to be sure we did not presume upon our clean linen of achievement. But in these last days I have wanted to stand on the house tops and proclaim, *Thank God there is a place known as the United States of America!* This is not arrogance. I speak with whatever humility there is within me. I have come to the place where I not only want this nation to endure as never before, but to have our loftiest ideals and achievements become the property of all mankind. And I have felt this more keenly since the "Cuba incident."

> O beautiful for patriot dream
>   That sees beyond the years
> Thine alabaster cities gleam,
>   Undimmed by human tears!
>   America! America!
>   God shed His grace on thee,
> And crown thy good with brotherhood
> From sea to shining sea.[2]

Aye! and to all the earth.

Let us be grateful on this national day of thanksgiving that religious motivation came into the human picture. I think I know how it came. As a professing Christian I have my faith as to how it came. You may think otherwise. However it came, let us be grateful. We have even taken

[2] Katharine Lee Bates.

note of this in our greatest national documents. "Endowed by their Creator" is one example, and there are many, many more. I happen to believe this "religious motivation" was no accident, that it is a gift of God. However this may be, I am glad it got into the nature and spirit of man. I am glad it made men capable of writing as did Edwin Markham:

> He drew a circle that shut me out—
> Heretic, rebel, a thing to flout.
> But Love and I had the wit to win:
> We drew a circle that took him in! [*]

I am thankful this motivation could lead a man like Thomas Jefferson, by no means an orthodox man, to state, "I have sworn upon the altar of God eternal hostility against every form of tyranny over the mind of man." I am grateful there could be a Francis of Assisi and a Dr. Tom Dooley and a Helen Keller and "millions though humble and nameless who the straight, hard pathway trod," all motivated by the deep resources of what I call God. The struggle referred to at the first was really not humanly contrived. And I am very grateful on our national day of thanksgiving in the year time ran out, *even* in the year time ran out, *especially* in the year time ran out, that such motivation is in the spirit of man. And being so, even from a possible burned out cinder, God forbid, once known as earth, the long climb could begin again. So let us indeed in this annual Thanksgiving celebration, declare with high faith and true purpose, "Bless the Lord, O my soul: and all that is within me, bless his holy name. Bless the Lord, O my soul, and forget not all his benefits."

[*] "Outwitted." Used by permission of Virgil Markham.

The Logistics of God

RICHARD C. HALVERSON

☆☆☆ One of the functions of the military which I have greatly admired yet always found incomprehensible is that called "logistics." I've never been able to understand how any man or group of men could manage such a coincidence of equipment, material, and people in the right way at the right time and the right place. I would like to think with you in terms of the logistics of God.

We are familiar with the golden text of the Bible—all of us memorized it as children: "God so loved the world, that he gave his only begotten Son, that whosoever believeth in him should not perish, but have everlasting life." (John 3:16.) This is the Christmas story in a word. The apostle Paul has taken this same profound truth and put it into different words which suggest the amazing logistics of redemption. I refer to the fourth verse of the fourth chapter of Galatians where Paul declares, "But when the fulness of the time was come, God sent forth his Son, made of a woman, made under the law." The apostle Paul had an amazing ability for stating profound truth in a very few simple words, and so he has done here. This uncomplicated little statement speaks to us first of the initiative of God.

Christmas is God's idea. Sometimes we are inclined to feel that it was man's the way we treat it; but history reminds us that Christmas is God's idea, not man's invention. As a matter of fact, nobody but God could have thought of Christmas, and our very abuses and misuses of it are evidence of that fact. For example, when man tries to invent some sort of a super being, he comes up with a Superman or a Captain Marvel. God gave the world a baby! The sheer uninventability of the Christmas narrative speaks of its Godly origin. Any author that could have created this plot would have been greater than the chief character about which he wrote.

The Advent Season testifies first to the initiative of God! I suppose that this is one of the hardest things for us to grasp at Christmastime, or any other time for that matter, the fact that God is continually on the initiative toward man. It is so easy for us to think of God as some far-off, aloof, indifferent, disinterested being, if he's a being at all; and often he is just an impersonal force who couldn't care less for the things that are happening in the cosmos not to mention the things that are happening in my life personally. The fact is that the Bible portrays a God who takes a personal interest in each of us. This is the high point of the Advent Season and Christmas. The Son of God made this very clear. With irresistible logic, he argued about the Father's care for us. He said, "Consider the lilies of the field, how they grow; they toil not, neither do they spin," yet your Heavenly Father takes care of them. Consider the birds of the air, a sparrow "shall not fall on the ground without your Father" in heaven knows of it; and you "are of much more value than many sparrows." As a matter of fact Jesus said, "The very hairs of your head are all numbered." The psalmist reminds us that not only are we known to God that way, but also the secret thoughts of our heart, the words yet unspoken on our tongue. He is the God of the cosmos. He is also the God of the atom. He is the God of the infinite, but he is also the God of the infinitesimal. He is the God of the telescope, but he is the God of the microscope. If the Scriptures mean anything, and if Christmas means anything to us, it is that God is interested in the microscopic, infinitesimal details of our lives. He knows about them, and he is concerned.

He cares! "When the fulness of the time" came, God did something. He is an active God, an interested God, a concerned God who has an answer.

The second fact of Christmas about which this verse speaks is the timing of God. "When the fulness of time was come . . ." Not before nor after but at the right moment the God who is perfect in his schedule acted. He is never too soon; he is never too late. The gears of God mesh perfectly in the divine economy.

There has never been a moment in history more propitious for the coming of the Son of God. Geographically, linguistically, politically, the time was ripe for the divine invasion. Rome had galvanized the world into one empire laced together by her amazing highway system; Greece had given the empire one language, and the Hebrews were restless for some kind of peaceful revolution. It was the "right time" for God to act in history.

Now this, too, is difficult for us to understand. We can appreciate how God does big things, and we can appreciate how God is in a sense incomprehensible: He knows everything, and he is all powerful, and so on. But it is not always easy to accept the fact that this God, who takes an active personal interest in each of us, times things perfectly. It is relatively easy to be committed to the purpose—the ultimate purpose of God—I suppose, just on the basis of logic and reason and sanity; that anyone will admit. Well, if there is a God and he does have a plan, obviously it is intelligent to conform to this plan. We see the sense in trusting the ultimate things which God, in believing that the *what* of God's will, the goal of God's will, the objective of God's will is with him; and we can rest in this. But the trouble with us is that we want it to happen right now.

We need to learn as Christian people that being committed to the will of God involves more than commitment to the what; it has to do with the *when* of God's will too. His timing is perfect. "When the fulness of the time was come, God . . ." You can trust God's timing. Peter is a vivid illustration of the man who, when he could not think of anything to say, said something anyway; and when he could not think of anything to do he did something. We are so much like that. It is difficult for us to learn the marvelous spiritual strategy of waiting upon the Lord. In the words of Isaiah, "They that wait upon the Lord shall renew their strength." Or,

"He that believeth shall not make haste." This is wisdom; this is sanity, to learn to be committed not only to the purpose of God's will but to the schedule. God's timing is right! We can depend upon it!

"When the fulness of the time was come, God sent forth his Son." Most wonderful of all about this plan of God was the answer, the solution, the gift. I suppose that God could have shouted from heaven so that the whole world could have heard him; he could have shouted ethics and ideology and philosophy, and even theology. God could have spoken from heaven day after day through the years and the centuries and the millenniums, making himself known generation by generation. But we might have misunderstood his language. God's answer to man's needs was not philosophy or ethics or an ideology or even a theology. God's answer was a babe! God's answer was a person. This we understand because we are people. God's answer is his Son.

You know there is a wide difference in knowing about a person and knowing a person. Not one of us here who does not know a great deal more about Abraham Lincoln than many of his most intimate friends knew about him. But they knew him and we only know about him. There is a great difference in knowing Jesus Christ and knowing about him, in knowing about God's Son and knowing him in personal experience.

Some years ago, while traveling on a plane down to Charlotte, North Carolina, I sat beside an IBM executive. In the course of our conversation I used the expression "knowing Christ." He said to me, "I'm interested in this phrase 'knowing Christ.'" "What do you mean when you say you know Christ?"

"Well," I said, "Tell me, do you have any close friends?"

"Yes, of course, I do."

"Name one of them." He named a man in Winston-Salem. I said, "He's a good friend?"

"He's one of the closest friends I've ever had in my life."

And I said, "Do you know him?"

"That's ridiculous. You just asked me if I had a friend. I told you one of my best friends. Of course, I know him. He's my friend."

"Now tell me what you mean when you say you know him." You know he could not tell me. He said, "Well, I-I-I mean—well I—when I say 'I know him' I—." So I prodded him a little bit. I said, "Does it mean you know how tall he is?"

"Well, as a matter of fact, I do. He's about five eleven and a half, but I don't mean that when I say I know him."

"Does it mean that you remember the color of his eyes?"

"No," he said, "I can't remember the color of his eyes."

"How about his hair?"

"It used to be brown, it's probably gray now. I haven't seen him for some time."

"Do you know where he was born and the circumstances of his birth, and of his early days?"

"As a matter of fact, I don't know where he was born and very little of his early days."

"Well," I said, "You say you know him, what do you mean then?"

He replied, "I can't say, but I know him and I know that I know him."

So it is with God's Son. He can be known, and you can know that you know him, but you will never be able to explain that relationship any better than my friend on the plane. This is the point of the Advent Season. To receive and know the gift of God which is his Son, born in a manger, grown to manhood, crucified on the cross, risen from the dead.

Does Christmas mean anything to you; or is it just a holiday, and after it is all over, will you just give a great sigh of relief and hope that the days will be long before it comes again? Does this season have eternal significance for you because you know Christ and know that you know him?

"When the fulness of the time was come, God sent forth his Son." God is everlastingly interested in you and me; everlastingly concerned. He everlastingly cares. God's timing is always perfect. No matter what the needs of your life may be or the circumstances, you can depend upon God's schedule, and God's answer is always God's Son.

God bless you.

In God Let Us Trust

BILLY GRAHAM

☆ ☆ ☆ During the past year we have all recalled the words of President Kennedy in which he said that the sword of Damocles hangs over the world. Damocles, who lived in the fourth century before Christ, once insulted King Dionysius of Syracuse. He was condemned by the king to attend a royal banquet and sit beneath a naked sword that was suspended by a single hair. We have been under such a sword. That sword was swinging back and forth and the hair was getting more frayed with every passing day.

We were told that we stood on the verge of a war that could mean the destruction of human race. And yet somehow through the aegis and the skill of our diplomats, war was averted. But I believe that something else happened. I am confident that in answer to the prayers of millions of people of all races around the world God Almighty intervened and saved us from the destruction of a war with modern weapons that can destroy much of the human race.

We have on our coins, "In God We Trust," and in our Pledge of Allegiance to the flag we say, "one nation, under God." We thank God for the chaplains in the armed forces who emphasize the moral and spiritual values of life to the men and women who serve their country today. This is all a part of the American heritage—a nation that believes in God, a nation that flies the Christian flag, a nation that believes in the providences of God in her national life.

Who of us can forget the picture of George Washington in prayer at Valley Forge, and then his taking his small army and routing the British, thus bringing about our victory in the war of the Revolution? Who can forget the words of Benjamin Franklin as he called the Constitutional Convention to prayer and out of that prayer meeting came the Constitution of the United States? Who can forget Abraham Lincoln and his cabinet on their knees many times during the Civil War, not praying for victory, but asking that God's will be done? Who can forget the great epochs in American life in which we have honored God and recognized God? I say that this is the secret of America's prosperity, America's strength, and this is the hope of America's future. But today, there are signs that we are beginning to loosen from our spiritual and moral mores. And I warn you that if that day ever comes, our nation is as doomed as was ancient Babylon or any of the other nations of history and antiquity that lost their faith in God.

In our country today we are facing gigantic problems on the moral and spiritual front. Pope Leo XIII once said, "When a society is perished, the true advice to give those that would restore it is to recall them to the principles from which it sprang." We see on every hand today a turning from God—a nation that is affluent and prosperous and yet a nation that sometimes serves God with its lips, but all too often God is not in their hearts. "In God We Trust" is written on our coins, but often not written in the depths of our souls. We need to be reminded of the words of Jesus Christ who warned the people of his day,

> [You] honor me with [your] lips,
> but [your] heart is far from me. (RSV.)

The great problem that the world faces today is not the race problem, not the Communist problem, not economic problems, but our great problem, as Dr. Waley said to the undergraduates at Cambridge, is "the heart problem." The heart problem is the heart of our problem because all of us suffer from heart disease—a spiritual heart disease. The Bible says, "All have sinned, and come short of the glory of God." The Bible says that the best of us are spiritual and moral failures. The Bible says that we fail to meet the requirements of God and that is the reason why we have so much sorrow, suffering, and trouble in the world.

This past year Marilyn Monroe took an overdose of sleeping pills. I have often wondered if her life might not have been spared had someone, under the proper circumstances, said to her, "There is spiritual help," "there is help for an empty soul."

Carl Jung, the great psychologist, has said that the central neurosis of our time is emptiness. We see people who are searching, thirsting, hungering for something to bring peace and joy and happiness in their personal lives and not finding it.

There is hope and that hope lies in Jesus Christ who was born of the Virgin Mary that first Christmas. The Scripture says, "Mary pondered these things in her heart." The angel said, "His name shall be called Jesus for he will save his people from their sins." And Paul said, "Christ Jesus came into the world to save sinners." We today are sinners. We need redemption and salvation. We may be the strongest military power in the world, but if we are resting on our military power alone to save us, we have a false security. To be relying upon anything except our faith in God is false security indeed.

Now this faith in God needs to be renewed. This faith in God needs to be restored. And it must start on the individual level. It must start with you. The people that help to direct the affairs of the greatest business in the world and the military security of the country have a tremendous responsibility. But without God's help, without the moral and spiritual strength that he gives, no military power is enough. Therefore, today, let us make this a time of renewal and of rededication. Let's make it a time in which we make a personal commitment to Christ, to God, to our Christian heritage, and to the principles that make this country great.

I've been on the battlefield and have held the hands of dying men. I have seen them in our hospitals, behind the front lines, and have watched them in their last hours. I have seen them die for these Stars and Stripes that we might have the freedoms we have today. Let us then rededicate ourselves as a people and as individuals to those principles and especially to the God whom we claim we trust.

Yes, you do have a need of Christ in your heart. The Bible says that man looks upon the outward appearance, but God looks upon the heart. If I could come into your homes and look into your hearts, what would I find? How about your home life? How about your personal life? What about the things down deep in your soul that nobody knows about except you and God? Jealousy? Pride? Envy? Prejudice? Hatred? Cheating? Lying? Ambitious, uncontrolled ego? What would be the things that God would find in your heart?

Helen Keller once said, "The best and most beautiful things in the world cannot be seen or touched but are just felt in the heart."

When Sir Walter Raleigh had laid his head upon the executioner's block, the officer asked if his head lay right. "It matters little, my friend, how the head lies provided the heart is right."

The Bible says, "The heart is deceitful above all things, and desperately wicked: who can know it?" Jesus said, "For out of the heart proceed evil thoughts, murders, adulteries, fornications, thefts, false witness, blasphemies."

What is God's attitude toward our hearts? The Bible says, "Shall not God search this out? for he knoweth the secrets of the heart." "I the Lord search the heart." "The Lord pondereth the hearts." Think of God Almighty, pondering your heart, examining your heart, weighing your heart, testing your heart. The heart stands for the total inner man—your mind, your conscience, your soul. God considers and evaluates, and he says, "How clean is your heart?"

The heart of the Christian faith is a Cross because Christ came to die. On that Cross his side was pierced, his body was broken, his blood was shed. When you come to a communion service you take of the bread that is symbolic of the body that was broken and the wine that is symbolic of the blood that was shed. On that Cross something mysterious and glorious happened. God took all of our sins and failures and mistakes and laid them on Christ. He bore our sins, he reconciled us to God, and now God says, "Because of Christ I can forgive you. I can wipe your sins out." But he says more than that—"I can give you a new capacity for living to face the problems and trials and difficulties of life. I can give you a new strength and a new power. In the midst of a crumbling world, in the midst of the possibilities of war I can give you security and peace and joy and rest." It is all yours! But you must receive God's offer of love and mercy.

The message of the Bible is the love of God. God says, "I love you." Will you receive that love? How do you receive it? You receive his love by repenting of your sins. That is not easy to do, because none of us likes to repent. We don't like to say we are wrong, and we don't like to humble ourselves and turn from our sins. But that is the requirement of God.

Then by simple faith we receive him as our Lord, Master, and Saviour. You can do that today. Right where you sit, right where you stand, you can make that great commitment. This, as far as you are personally concerned, would be the climactic event of the ages. This for you would be the turning point between death and life, between heaven and hell. This could be a moment in which you would become a different man and a different woman and God would go with you from this hour on.

That is America's heritage. That was the faith of some of our great men of the past. Abraham Lincoln said, "When I left Springfield I asked the people to pray for me. I was not a Christian. When I buried my son, the severest trial of my life, I was not a Christian. When I went to Gettysburg, I then and there consecrated myself to Christ."

Something happened to Lincoln at Gettysburg. Something could happen to you today that could change and transform your life and make you the kind of American citizen that we need at this hour of our history in which the responsibilities are far greater than we can bear without the help of God.

Shall we pray: Our Father and our God we pray that in this moment in the quietness and the deepest recesses of our soul and heart, we will surrender all to Christ and make him our Lord and Master and Saviour, for we ask in his name. Amen.

The Challenge of Freedom

JOHN C. BROGER

☆☆☆ The twentieth century has been a period of great changes in the areas of increased political awareness in the newly emerging nations, great social upheavals such as are occurring in Latin America and the Far East, and tremendous strides in mass communications as witnessed by the exploration of space and the tremendous propaganda barrages waged among various groups of nations. During this turbulent and trying period not the least of these changes and perhaps the greatest is in the realm of personal values and spiritual convictions. The spiritual compass of life is the only sure guide by which a man may chart his pathway through life. All other change, dynamic as it may be, leads in false directions if the spiritual compass is deflected or influenced by purely materialistic values.

Our lives today are set in the most dramatic conflict of values and convictions yet recorded in history. The compass which charts the course of life for millions of people may swing between that world of personal free choice which is the specific gift of God and that world of suppression and slavery known to this age as international communism.

156

Across the nation, committed Christian Americans are becoming increasingly concerned with their role in the cold war. Not only have Christian Americans become aroused at home, but reports from many missionaries worldwide have indicated growing Communist pressures in countries where they minister. Particularly is this true in newly emerging nations where men and women for the first time in the world's history are recognizing that the vast gulfs of prejudice and injustice can be overcome, and that freedom and justice under law can establish a life where each man and his family is able to believe and work and live according to the dictates of conscience.

On the other hand, strident voices of some anti-Communist leaders have left Christians with a new sense of awareness, motivation, and even fear, but with little or no understanding of the multitude of Christian answers to the false premises and concepts of Communist ideology. This unfortunate lack of understanding of how the Communists exploit the sympathy of Christian idealism abroad with anti-colonial and anti-clerical slogans of the Communist movement has even in some cases led unwary victims to identify themselves with the Communist Party. Most of us recognize that communism is bad, that it is a false religion, and that it jeopardizes the freedom of all individuals as well as nations. We talk about the battle for the hearts and minds of men. How do you fight this kind of battle? What weapons do you use? What principles, values, and concepts are at stake? Most of us rarely worry about the definitions of these words.

We speak about fighting for freedom or the American way of life. We talk about our way of life as in conflict with the Communist way of life. What does this kind of battle entail? Why are we involved in it? Why should we be more than casually concerned? Why not let government do it or the military or the Congress? After all, some say, don't we elect our representatives in government to watch out for this sort of problem?

There should be no question as to why the Department of Defense is concerned today about the convictions, ideals, motivations, loyalties or any other of those intangible qualities which appear to be a major contest area in this latter part of the twentieth century. Out of approximately 1,500,000 Americans scattered in almost every section of the world, there are about 800,000 military, 600,000 of their dependents, 30,000 civilian government personnel, and 70,000 persons of non-government organizations overseas. Roughly the ratio of defense personnel overseas to other Americans on business is fourteen to one.

What the citizen-soldier of today believes, the depths of his loyalty, the knowledge of his enemy, the toughness of his character—all these things and more may well determine the effectiveness of our national will to resist. Tremendous resources of money, time, and effort are expended in training men in the use of modern tactical weapons and in measuring the effectiveness of this training. The importance of this technical know-how cannot be underrated, but of great significance as well in this period of decision is the spirit and will needed to use effectively this tactical knowledge if or when "the chips are down."

Present Communist strategy views the role of man to be more vital than ever. According to Khrushchev, "The Communist reform of society is inalienably linked with the upbringing of a new man, who must harmoniously combine spiritual wealth, moral purity, and physical perfection. The Communist man of tomorrow will be free from the unworthy characteristics derived from an exploiting regime, private property egoism, and the desire to live at the expense of other people's labor, petty bourgeoisism, and the like."

My basic question is this, if the Soviets are able to continue their present tactics successfully over the next decade, will our nation and our fighting forces consisting of today's and tomorrow's youth retain the will to resist Soviet aggression? If the answer is in the affirmative; if we are of the opinion that our present methods are successful and satisfactory; if we are convinced that the Soviet "new man" concept is a mythical farce, then the problem is vastly simplified. If, on the other hand, there is even a doubt concerning the image which we feel is essential to our nation and the U.S. citizen-soldier, then we must assume that our responsibilities place upon all of us an obligation to plan and promote a program which will support a responsible citizen-soldier concept and all that it implies.

The protagonist of communism has been carefully trained and developed into a highly skilled technician, utilizing the very spiritual ideals and truths of Christianity in a reverse process. First he has been taught how to analyze and exploit every disagreement, discrimination, and injustice in any part of organized society. Second, he has been taught how to fan further the flame of these exploitable and highly combustible grievances in order to dismember each lawful means to correct any such grievance. Even though his own conviction is based on atheistic, materialistic Marxism, the success of his penetration into local community affairs depends upon his ability to evaluate properly the basic desires, needs, and hopes of his target audience. In many cases his appeal for the accomplishment of his devious purposes will be to the baser qualities of human nature such as greed, bitterness, lust for power, hatred, and any number of variations of ungodly characteristics.

If the Communist agitator dealt only through such evil practices, the problem would not be nearly so difficult. The fact is, however, that he poses in most cases as an angel of light. His chief tool in the complex of Communist penetration machinery lies in offering the solution of Socialist revolution to achieve freedom from every injustice, every prejudice, and every discrimination. This spurious appeal is tailored in each case by the Communist technician to exploit a problem where personal freedom under law is not available. There are other Communist tools as well in his subversive kit. This appeal, however, to the legitimate desires, hopes, and aspirations of mankind is the most powerful.

The Christian must know the basic, God-given, inalienable rights necessary to the well-being of a free people. He must know not only what they are, but how they should be protected. For lack of knowledge in this vital area provides the beginning for the Communist technician of subversion. The Christian needs to know his individual responsibility to maintain liberty and every lawful means to defend it. He needs to know in detail what will happen if these freedoms are lost; for once lost the power and force of Communist machinery and domination allow them to return no more without violence and blood shed, if at all.

Throughout the history of civilization men have had different ideas of liberty. Plato and Aristotle associated liberty with justice or giving every man his due. The Epicureans thought of liberty as complete freedom to pursue pleasure and to avoid pain. The Stoics and later Thomas Aquinas and John Locke held that man possessed natural rights which derive from natural law. The exercise of these rights constitutes liberty. The German philosopher, Immanuel Kant, held that liberty is connected with moral law. Human freedom involves the necessity of doing one's duty as dictated by the moral conscience. There can be seen here the Christian influence upon the structure of governmental philosophy. To do freely what one ought to do is the true expression of human dignity and moral responsibility. In these modern days, liberty is regarded as the freedom of the individual to think his own thoughts and to speak and act as he thinks proper, subject only to the restrictions necessary to preserve the liberty of other individuals and the good of society. Here then is organized society's application to Christ's admonition, "Thou shalt love thy neighbor as thyself." Here also is a thread of biblical truth running through the various philosophies of men who expounded on the nature and structure of government.

Western civilization is rooted and grounded on the Christian foundation. The cornerstone of this foundation was the Judaic religious tradition which believed in the universality of God, the reign of law, and the respect for the freedom and dignity of the individual. Moses the lawgiver of Israel died about twelve hundred years before Christ, many centuries before the Golden Age of Greece. The laws given by Moses are the ethical foundations on which all democracies since the decline of Rome have rested. Most of the "thou shall nots" of the Ten Commandments are also the "thou shall nots" of present-day democratic governments. Throughout the Old Testament are found commands and injunctions which safeguard the liberties of the people and denunciations of those who defy the will of God by tyranny and oppression. "Proclaim liberty throughout all the land and unto all the inhabitants thereof" is commanded in Lev. 25:10. Thousands of years later it was inscribed by our founding fathers upon the Liberty Bell as a reminder of our heritage. Leviticus also enjoins equality before the law for all peoples, citizens, and foreigners alike, "Ye shall have one manner of law, as well for a stranger, as for one of your own country"; and tolerance is affirmed with, "Ye shall not therefore oppress one another." Jesus in the Gospels constantly emphasized the direct relation of the individual to God and the infinite worth of the human personality. The teachings of Jesus, embodied in the Golden Rule, provided an additional foundation stone in the practical working of the self-disciplines necessary to liberty under law. Paul in his epistle to the Galatians proclaimed brotherhood in Christ and the equality of all peoples with,

"There is neither Jew nor Greek, there is neither bond nor free, there is neither male nor female: for ye are all one in Christ Jesus."

Even though governments and decrees existed before the Mosaic Law, mankind waited until the codes and laws of justices were given by God to Moses before a government was established in which man participated under the guidance and influence of God. Today the U. S. Constitution can be considered an historical example of such a contract. In effect, this makes the Golden Rule, or as the apostle James called it "the royal law according to the Scriptures," a contract by which men legally bound themselves together in a form of government. The Bill of Rights may be looked upon as the royal law of our Constitution.

Because God intended that man, created in his image, should exercise the ability of conscience to distinguish between right and wrong, man has the capacity to set forth guides to distinguish between what on the one hand is good or beneficial for each and all and what, on the other hand, is bad in the sense of being hurtful to both the individual and the community. The problem of ultimate spiritual values, based upon specific biblical concepts, cannot be sidestepped in any honest attempt to assess political and social ideas. God never, on the one hand, intended man to be an automated robot, merely responding to the pressure of certain buttons which would propel him in this or that direction. Neither, on the other hand, did he intend that man should be a product of chaotic anarchy without restraint, without a discipline which he is capable of imposing upon himself, or without a clear-cut spiritual purpose for life without which man is but a predatory animal, devouring the weaker species in order to survive himself.

By definition, the state is a large group of people occupying definite territory, organized under a government, and possessing sovereignty and independence. Government is the organ of the state for social control. Sovereignty is the power of the state to enforce its will within the borders of the state. The will of the state is expressed in law. Thus it may be seen how important it is for the God-man-government relationship to exist in proper perspective each to the other. There is need for man to call upon God and there is also a need for God to deal in the affairs of man and his political entity—the state. Without this, government itself becomes predatory.

The U.S. Constitution in order to maintain the principles of Christian liberty added a Bill of Rights guaranteeing the rights of individuals and at the same time establishing a firm separation between church and state. But with our Bill of Rights we also must assume personally a commensurate Bill of Responsibilities. These are the two essential elements of individual liberty, freedom in balance with responsibility.

Our Constitution is a landmark in the age-long struggle for the liberty of the individual, the free choice of the individual, and the opportunity for self-discipline which God intended for man. In this document, hewn and shaped to the spiritual concepts of biblical truths, are contained all the guarantees of Christian freedoms. It is our shield and armor so long as its provisions prevail and so long as the majority of our peoples sustain a belief in, and an adherence to, the great truths from which this document has drawn its strength and significance.

The trials and tests through which Abraham Lincoln passed in the preservation of these liberties led him to say:

Let every American, every lover of liberty, every well-wisher to his posterity swear by the blood of the revolution never to violate in the least particular the laws of the country, and never to tolerate their violation by others. As the patriots of '76 did to the support of the Declaration of Independence, so to the support of the Constitution and laws let every American pledge his life, his property, and his sacred honor. Let every man remember that to violate the law is to trample on the blood of his father, and to tear the charter of his own and his children's liberty. . . . Let it be taught in schools, in seminaries, and in colleges, let it be written in primers, in spelling books and in Almanacs, let it be preached from the pulpit, proclaimed in legislative halls, and enforced in courts of justice. And, in short, let it become the political religion of the nation, and, in particular, a reverence for the Constitution.

We must always remember that a great part of our spiritual armor depends on our attitude toward the importance and significance of the individual human being. The Scripture has said that one person is worth the whole world. If we believe it and if we practice it—in a nation under God—our defense is sure.

The Doom and Renewal of Civilization

CHARLES MALIK

☆ ☆ ☆ Nothing is easier today than to dwell pathetically on the elements of doom and disaster. The grounds of discouragement are so numerous that it takes at times a violent wrenching of the spirit to wake up to the real elements of hope and renewal. It is good to analyze and criticize and face the ugly facts, and not to face them in truth and honesty would be a terrible sin. But analysis would also become a terrible sin if it landed us in despair while we still believed in the creative powers of man and God. And the facts, especially if taken in their totality and seen in the right perspective, are not as ugly as some gloomy minds are in the habit of painting them. Far from disaster being the inevitable issue of the present trend of things, it is altogether possible that humanity is on the verge of a new age, as wonderful in its brilliance as completely unknown as yet in its character. The present moment therefore tests at once our ability to see the obvious truth without blinking and our ability to see the deeper truth of faith without doubting.

Who is not troubled today by the great strain which the family is undergoing under the complex conditions of modern life—parents often pulled in different directions, parents not having enough time to see and love and play with their children?

Who has not wondered at the inordinate spread of juvenile delinquency in modern society?

Who has not noticed or suffered from the general collapse of morals in the world—standards of integrity, honesty, purity, truth no longer holding, the soul being ready not only to yield to temptation without resisting, but at times even actively to seek occasions of temptation itself?

Who has not made telling observations on the effect of the machine on the human mind and on the whole tone and character of contemporary civilization?

Who has not lamented the fullness, drabness, mechanicalness, and unnaturalness of urban existence—this existence which is spreading all over the world at a terrific rate—and who has not time and again longed to return to the simple life of nature?

Who is not infected by the general malaise of nervousness, hecticness, movement, meaninglessness, absence of peace, and grace and rest for the poor and tormented human soul?

In the social sphere, who is not upset by the disregard for human rights and fundamental freedoms and by the consequent eruption of unreason and violence to assert these rights?

Who is not profoundly disturbed by the phenomenal spread of communism in recent decades—by its holding in its iron grip one-third of mankind today and its softening, infiltrating, and intimidating in varying degrees the remaining two-thirds?

Who is not perplexed by the apparent impotence of the free world to push back or even at times to resist this incredible Communist onslaught?

Who has not perceived in his own life and in the life of society an increasing emphasis on materialism, secularism, and relativism—an emphasis serving as the ideal spiritual preparation for an eventual Communist takeover?

Who is not dismayed by the constant shrinkage of the domain of freedom—the mind of man being more and more subjected to arbitrary and tyrannical systems?

Who is not frustrated by the recent political and military reverses and by the apparently insufficient progress in certain sectors of economics and technology?

Who does not live in fear of war—the unimaginable holocaust of the atom?

Who is not paralyzed in his planning—the future being so uncertain, so mysterious, so inscrutable?

And as a result of all this, who is not entertaining some doubt at least as to whether Western civilization can much longer endure—with communism attacking it at every point from without, with fear, softness, and uncertainty undermining it from within, and with the neutralist world at least indifferent to its fate?

There is no dearth, therefore, of grounds for discouragement and frustration. He who dwells only on these things and what they imply must conclude that civilization is doomed. The company of the Spenglers and Toynbees has lately increased, I mean those who affect the knowledge of a law of growth and decay according to which civilizations develop and decline. These people for the most part live in their ideas and not in the world. According to these theories, civilizations, like individuals age, and when the end comes they must die and fresh civilizations will arise on their debris. This impersonal, cyclic determinism goes back to pagan thought, both Greek and Oriental. It antedates and lies outside the heart of the Christian message, the message which insists that nature, decay, corruption, and death can never be the last word. Marxism essentially belongs to the same type of impersonal, non-Christian thought. Theories of the most ingenious character are devised by these outlooks to prove that Western civilization has exhausted itself, that immanent in its development has been an inexorable law of decay, that this law operates completely independently of the human will, and that the end is not far off when, fatigued and unable to revive itself, Western civilization lays down its burden and other youthful shoulders carry on the torch. These theories, suggestive and erudite as they may be, nevertheless forget two decisive things: the freedom of man and the mystery of God. Through his freedom there is no impersonal law of history that man cannot rise above and alter, and through his mystery there is no law of death that God, in his freedom, cannot overcome.

I shall therefore indicate in the briefest possible terms the main lines of thought which, in my opinion, constitute the real grounds of hope, and which will, when fully developed, demonstrate that far from doom being the fate of civilization it is probably renewal that is just around the corner.

The West contains the greatest concentration by far of science, technology, and industry in the world. These things are rooted in a cumulative tradition that extends for thousands of years. They are also self-perpetuating. They represent much more than mere mechanical technique; they represent a fundamental theoretical attitude of a whole culture toward nature, man, and history, an attitude that cannot be transplated to other cultures overnight. With Germany and Japan securely on the Western side and with science and technology developing as they are in the West, there is no reason to believe that any comparable concentration will arise anywhere else in the world for at least another century. In the space of a century of scientific and technological superiority in which the mind is truly alerted to the ultimate issues of destiny, much indeed can be assured.

This is so far as science and nature and the harnessing of nature's forces are concerned. What about man and culture and history? The dimension of history is now more fully disclosed to the inquiring mind than ever before. And, incidentally, it is the canons of Western scholarship itself that have opened this majestic dimension of the past—not only of the Western past but of every past. It is almost literally true that the past, in its fundamental structures, is now a completely open book. One need not fear that there is a great deal still hidden that will, when uncovered one day, truly astound the world. There will be endless refinements, but the basic contributions are known at least in part. Let every living culture therefore display its full achievements. In the total array of cultures and civilizations that can thus be fathomed, Western civilization, rooted as it is in Greece, Rome, the Near East, the Mediterranean, and Western Europe, stands out as something quite unique. In its unbroken continuity for four thousand years or more, in the creative principles of thought and feeling it established, in the patient disclosure of the mystery of God which it has inherited and which it can never disown, in the incomparable products of beauty and reflection and worship and political wisdom and collective endeavor which it has deposited, it need not feel any sense of inferiority with respect to any other civilization whatsoever.

In fact all other civilizations have learned and continue to learn from it, far more than it has any need to learn from them. This is its distinctive universal and humane character; namely, its preoccupation with truth, the truth that is valid for all, and its concentration upon man as the origin, center, and end of everything. He who, placing himself above any silly political or diplomatic considerations in order to see the truth in itself and for its own sake, penetrates to the depths of achievement of Western civilization, has no doubt whatever about its infinite sources of strength. The only question is whether those of its children who have been initiated into its deepest mysteries are going to prove worthy of what they have received and known.

The total forces of the West have not been fully committed. This is most important. Should the occasion arise for the total commitment of these forces, who can predict the outcome? Every time this happened in the past, the West came out in the end victorious. Let the West as a whole really feel the pinch, and then I doubt whether anything can stand in its way. Having regard to its infinite potentialities of mind, morals, and material, and to the creative potency of freedom, I do not have the slightest doubt that the enemies of God, man, and freedom will not have the last word—no matter how much suffering the resistance and destruction of them will entail.

There is a remarkable awakening in America as to the issues and dangers involved. This has never happened before in peacetime. People seem to me to be ready for any eventuality; they only ask to be told what is expected of them. It is quite possible that in many respects the people are ahead of their leaders. I feel that in a matter of days, if not hours, they could be galvanized into the most heroic action. A civilization that is thus alert and ready cannot be said to be nearing its end.

This raises the question of co-ordination. The greatest danger is unco-ordinated individualism, the frittering away of effort, the non-convergence of energy and interest onto a single point, onto a unitary outcome. People are excited, they sense the danger, they want to join in some common effort, they crave to know what that common effort is; but so far nobody has told them, nobody has summoned them to a supreme effort for the common good. A man, demanding that he be shown the way yet appearing to wait indefinitely without anybody showing him the way, soon develops a terrible inner frustration. If Western civilization goes down, it will only be because its leadership has failed to show it the way. There is no impersonal law of growth and decay here at work whatsoever. There is the very personal moral failure of the leaders to show the way. *And a real way out most certainly there is.* The actual, ready potentialities of this civilization in every sphere are so tremendous, so overpowering, that with the proper co-ordination and the right voice of leadership it can rise to any challenge. The greatest danger today is that either this leadership is not forthcoming or its voice will come too late.

The fervor and dedication with which the great peoples of Asia, Africa, and Latin America are renewing their life are matters of the greatest satisfaction. Only good can come out of this peaceful renewal. They are fully entitled to the opportunity of enjoying the natural right to be themselves in freedom; namely, to fall back upon themselves, to search their own souls, to discover the grounds of their native dignity, and thus to enter anew into the dynamics and responsibilities of history. An order of equality and mutual respect and appreciation should prevail. It is far better and healthier to be dealing with moral equals than with inferiors or superiors, because that is the order of freedom in which nothing can be taken for granted and you should always be on the alert. That is why I regard the rise of the East as being not cause for alarm and doom of the West but ground for its renewal. You can really be at your best only in the company of moral equals. There is no relaxation any more with the East questioning and challenging the West at its deepest. A genuine renewal is not when you renew yourself while the rest of the world remains snoring; a genuine renewal can only be an organic part of the total renewal of all.

I do not despair of Russia and the West reaching some kind of an agreement. Of course this will not happen while communism, which as a total world outlook contradicts all the fundamental values of the West, rules the Russians. I am not at all thinking of communism versus capitalism here; I am thinking of communism as a religion, as an absolute materialistic, atheistic interpretation of man, society, history, and the final things. But I trust the Russian people, on the basis of their own creative background, to see in their own day the sham and falsehood of this outlook and thus to rid themselves of its yoke. I have a great faith in the Russian spirit performing this miracle one day. This can come about only if the West does not let the Russian people down, either by hating them, or by identifying them with the Communist Party, or by ceasing to commune with them on every possible level, or by failing to appreciate their great spiritual genius, or by itself turning materialistic and forgetting about its great spiritual heritage. But should the Russians rid themselves of communism and return to their wonderful original spirituality (and no return can ever be to the same position), and should they live in full spiritual and temporal peace with the rest of the world, then I should like to see the despairing spirits who prophesy the doom of Western civilization. These spirits seem to me to be praying that such a fundamental understanding does not take place. But a genuine reconciliation between Russia and the West, certainly not on the basis of communism but on the basis of a renewed Russia that has purged herself of communism, could bring about the greatest renewal of Western civilization in its history. A whole new epoch for the whole of humanity, absolutely wonderful in its promise, will then dawn. Such a thing is not impossible, and its mere possibility disproves any silly determinism with respect to the fate of Western civilization.

One must never underestimate the power of freedom. It is most significant that the great expression of the freedom of man which we find in *Doctor Zhivago* scared the communists out of their wits all over the world. One must keep the torch of freedom burning—in his soul, in his country, before the world. The children of freedom little know what a world-shaking and world-transforming weapon they can wield. Only they must not let material values overwhelm the wonderful spiritual values of freedom. It is original freedom that creates all economic and material values, and these can never by themselves create freedom. The fate of the world hangs on the extent to which the West shall remain actively faithful to the creative freedom which is at the base of all that is true and good and beautiful and graceful and holy in all civilization.

I am encouraged by the diverse movements for church unity. The Protestants appear to be getting closer together, and I consider the decision of the Presbyterians to seek unity with three other Protestant groups an historic decision. A major theme of the Third Assembly of the World Council of Churches meeting in New Delhi was this question of unity. The Ecumenical Council which the Pope called on the subject of unity testifies to a new spirit animating Rome today. The Orthodox all over thirst for unity and communion, and the Russian Orthodox Church's decision to join the World Council of Churches must be interpreted as a sincere expression of this thirst. What is most encouraging in all these gropings, from my point of view, is that the principle sought is not a watering down of faith and doctrine, but a decided return to a new orthodoxy. The problems are still insuperable, but we are dealing here not with what is impossible with man but with what is possible to God. Let the Christians really constitute One Body, or at least let them in perfect charity, come appreciably closer together, and you do not then need to worry at all about the fate of civilization. The Christians cannot sit back and carp at their political leaders; they are even more responsible than these leaders for the fate of their civilization; they, even more than the politicians, must assume full responsibility for what the future holds in store.

The new spiritual leavening is further evidenced by the widespread intense interest in the Bible, in liturgy, in the sacraments, in fundamental theology, and in the original tradition. If you compare what the seminaries now teach and produce with the silly and superficial rationalism and liberalism and humanism and psychologism which dominated them only a generation ago, you think you are dealing with two different ages altogether. The unfathomable mystery of God is again impinging on the dull mind of man with incalculable consequences precisely for the fate of civilization itself.

Civilization is the joint creation of God and man; it is a human-divine artifact. The very essence of God is freedom, and man, insofar as he is human, participates in the divine essence. Therefore it is nonsense, on strict metaphysical grounds, to speak of civilization subject to the iron laws of fate. Through the free action of God and man every decay can be arrested and every civilization can be redeemed. Those who talk of the doom of civilization may not have known the renewing power of God in their own lives. And those who know this power know also that one man thus renewed may save the whole world.

In addressing civilized and learned audiences one is not supposed to mention Jesus Christ. Such a mention shocks and disturbs. Rather one is supposed to dissolve Christ into generalities, ideas, principles. And so one had better talk of "spiritual values" or "religious principles" or at most "Christian truths." But the greatest thing about any civilization is the human person, and the greatest thing about this person is the possibility of his encounter with the Person of Jesus Christ. With your permission therefore I shall not dissolve Christ into principles and generalities.

When we speak of a thing we mean primarily its essence. Certainly Jesus Christ, the Church, the Cross belong to the essence of Western civilization. Whatever is doomed, *these* are not doomed; on the contrary, they doom everything else. The renewal of Western civilization is guaranteed so long as Jesus Christ remains at its heart. Let it forsake him, and forthwith it dooms itself. And to the extent it has forsaken him and he is no longer at its heart, it has doomed itself.

He who is living—and living here means the life of responsibility and decision, the life in which you cannot have everything but you must decide in favor only of one alternative and ruthlessly and responsibly destroy a number of alternatives—and not only thinking and philosophizing in this age certainly must feel that things are passionately straining toward an event to come. This is a preeminently eschatological age. There is a sense in which everything is now groaning, travailing, waiting, expecting something to come! If you do not feel this in your bones, you are not living in this age. In the end an act of divine intervention is necessary to precipitate and crystallize the whole thing. A day of judgment, I assure you, is at hand. We should never expect anything less than the face of God himself, renewing and replenishing the face of the earth.

An intense personal existence, like that of David, in which the struggle against the devil and his forces is carried to the nth degree in the presence of God; an existence therefore whose personal suffering is not wasted, but is wonderfully redeemed by the Cross; an existence which is never passive, but is most active in its waiting on the Lord; an existence which, because it knows God, believes in miracles—real, not imaginary, not sentimental, miracles—and expects them; an existence which is straining every nerve toward a fundamental spiritual breakthrough, a breakthrough not only of man to God but above all of God to man: this kind of existence is still perfectly possible to those who will be born anew, regardless of their rigidity and regardless of their age. It will be rewarded by the freedom and mercy of God, with a new outpouring of the Holy Spirit which will transform the face of the earth—this earth of sorrow and tears, this earth of suffering and estrangement, this earth of misunderstanding and pain, this earth of narrowness and greed, this earth of loneliness and rebellion, this earth which has willfully separated itself from God.

To all of us in our several callings let me assure you that every generation from the beginning of time is envying you. It is the greatest honor to be alive today. You may be destined to play a decisive role in the certain coming renewal of civilization.

Therefore face your historic task with the utmost expectancy. Trust in the living God. Remember that he is pleased only with the humble. Believe in freedom. Wish it and work for it for all. Be strong in the right. Love your fellowmen. Never weary in serving them. Never betray the deepest in your heritage. Never turn to strange, new gods. Treat yourselves always with a sense of humor. And so live and suffer as to be always ready to face your Maker, always asking his forgiveness and always thanking him from the bottom of your heart.

Our Mission Today

JOHN WESLEY LORD

☆ ☆ ☆ We are living today at the beginning of a new age in which the securities and religious concepts of the past are changing and new securities and new concepts must be found. Never have the rewards for right decisions and the penalties for wrong decisions been more swift or momentous. The times are dark, crime is rampant, and sin is heinous. But to the Christian God is strong. "Neither death, nor life, nor angels, nor principalities, nor powers, nor things present, nor things to come, nor height, nor depth, nor any other creature, shall be able to separate us from the love of God which is in Christ Jesus our Lord."

Despite this great affirmation of the Christian, there are many for whom the light has run out. The late Ernie Pyle at the end of his remarkable life in a letter to a friend wrote, "If you have any light send some my way. God knows I've run out of light."

The late Munich clown, Karl Vallentin, once enacted the following scene: The curtain rises on a stage which is totally dark except for a small circle of light cast by a solitary street lamp. Vallentin, with a long-drawn and deeply worried face, walks round and round in the circle of light, searching desperately for something. "What have you lost?" asks a policeman who has entered the scene.

"The key to my house," replies Vallentin.

The policeman joins in the search until, after awhile finding nothing, he asks, "Are you sure you lost it here?"

"No," answers Vallentin, pointing to a dark corner of the stage, "Over there."

"Then why on earth are you looking for it here?"

"There's no light over there," says Vallentin. This tragic-comic drama serves quite well to illustrate the cosmic crisis in which so many people are living today, and it is in such an hour that the church must speak with relevance and with power.

However, in this new age the church must also take into account some new facts, for the mission of the church is in part determined by the nature of the world in which it finds itself. There are many promising signs in the new age, and yet they are fraught with danger. First we note the emergency of a promising yet dangerous technological world. The technology of the world in which we live is not against God. These wonderful new developments are neither good nor bad in themselves, it all depends on the use that man makes of them. Also we must face the decline of the Western world from its place of dominance. And with this decline of the Western world has come the emergence of the independent nations of Asia and Africa. In eighteen years 800,000,000 people have gained political independence. Another fact which the church must face is the rise of the Communist states. One third of the human race is now under the domination of communism. Threatening the complacency of the past are the new relationships among world religions. Hinduism, Buddhism, and Islam are now making claim as world religions. While today one out of three are Christian, we know that by the year 2000 only one out of five will be Christian. And yet paralleling this new trend of non-Christian religions has also come the emergence of the worldwide Christian church. This is all part of the new age. What are we as churchmen to say about it, and what is God doing within it? We must ask ourselves if the God that we worship is big enough for the new age into which we have moved?

A further word should be said about what is happening to Christians in certain parts of the world. While in the States we have the picture of a Christian church that is growing and thriving, in many parts of the world the church has been placed on the defensive. This is particularly true in China. Here we are told that Christians have been humbled by the dedication of disciplined young Communists with whom they have had to work. They have also been frightened by these same Communists and some Christians have been killed. Christians have for the first time in recent years experienced disgrace. In 1950 the Communists put out a classified list of workers in society and the two at the bottom were prostitutes and missionaries. Indeed it ought to be said that prostitutes were placed one rung higher than the missionaries. Many of these Christians in foreign lands have been isolated, the churches have been weakened, some of the Christians have been silenced, and to our shame, some have been manipulated by the Communists. There will be many battles that we must fight in this new world with those who would exclude Christ.

However dark this picture, the Christian church stands as the great bulwark of the freedoms of humanity. Here let me say a word about the significance of the chaplains in the armed services and the churches which they are conducting on the various installations, bases, and posts throughout the world. In a sense this is the church in dispersion. Perhaps the chaplains in the armed services have more to say to the church at home than the church at home has to say to them. They are in the main stream of this fast-changing life and are helping to determine the new direction that stream is to take in the future life of mankind. In a sense they have become the navigators. The church at home has come to recognize that it is a dangerous thing to live in a neighborhood that is not a brotherhood. But it has found it difficult to put this realization into practice. I think significantly they have been far more successful in their work throughout the world than some of the churches at home have been.

Against this sordid background, however, we dare to make the claim that Jesus Christ is the Center to which all men must turn if they are to find meaning within the emerging world civilization. This is the gospel that we proclaim. The church dares to say that it has the power to match every sordid fact of the human dilemma with the faith of a divine solution. This can and will be done if the church will stand in this hour true to its primary task. The church must be the voice of conscience of human society convicting men of their sin. It must wield the weapons of the spirit and remain loyal to Jesus Christ. It must make itself responsible for good legislation and destroy the myth of the superman. The church dares to declare that the primary problems of our day are not military but spiritual, and in this area the work of the church will be tested.

The Christian today sees the wonderful works of God being manifest. He sees these works being manifest in this world of frightening technological development. He sees men and nations sincerely working to secure a just and lasting peace for mankind, and they are working not in despair but in a spirit of hopefulness that the very crisis has forced upon us. We must co-operate to live. We will co-operate or die. We have every reason to believe that the time will come when through heroic effort and sincere commitment to Christian life and principle a better world will be secured for mankind. The church believes that it has the power to provide a humanizing influence as the nations of the world deal with automation, urbanization, problems of race, and world responsibility. This is the great new missionary frontier, and these are the borders that must be crossed, even as our fathers crossed geographical borders a hundred years ago. It has been said that the mission of the church today is in these new areas and that it is harder to be a Christian in the United States of America than in any other place in the world. But we have the power, and will provide the changes that must be wrought.

The Christian sees the wonderful works of God taking place in his church. A new and greater church is being born. Here again the chaplains and the military can lead the way in this great ecumenical movement. A critic of the church likened the church to an African kraal, a sheltered place surrounded by a thorny hedge designed to keep the family safely sheltered within and undesirables and animals without. But this was quickly countered by one who said, "No, the church today resembles rather a supply depot for parachute jumpers."

The church is mission.

> Where cross the crowded ways of life,
> Where sound the cries of race and clan,

> Above the noise of selfish strife,
> We hear Thy voice, O Son of man.[1]

This is the faith of the church. The voice will be heard, and the voice will also be heeded.

The Christian, of course, sees something of the wonderful power of God within himself, and he knows that at all times he has the power to become a child of God. A recent urban development worker said that one of the hardest lessons he had to learn was that "decent, safe and sanitary housing did not produce decent, safe and sanitary people." But the gospel that we proclaim has the power to change indecent, unsafe, and unsanitary people into the very sons of God. We start at the place where God seems to be absent but with the assurance and hope that he must be there if one stays long enough. It is true that these are dark days, dark days for the world and dark days for the church. The church does not despair but rejoices that it has been challenged by this kind of age and this kind of need for the church has seen once again that it is mission. It is not an institution. It is not a creed or doctrine. It is mission. It is life being spent to meet the need of mankind.

In the fourteenth chapter of the book of Exodus we have the story of a dark day for the Israelites but in this wonderful record God said to Moses, "Speak unto the children of Israel, that they go forward." The Israelites were pursued by the Egyptians; the people had lost heart and blamed Moses for it all. But God was there. Moses stretched forth his hand, the sea divided and the Israelites crossed, and the Egyptians were lost. So today, despite the darkness of the hour, we celebrate the wonderful works of God. So long as the church remembers that it is mission it has nothing to fear, and when it ceases to care for itself and is willing to give up its life for humanity, it will know its grandest hour. I covet for the men in the armed forces the opportunities they have in distant points of the world to make manifest a gospel that can save to the uttermost. Let the church be the voice of conscience in human society everywhere, convicting men of their sin; let it wield the weapons of the spirit and remain loyal to Jesus Christ. Let it make itself responsible for good legislation and the future will be secure.

[1] "Christ in the City" by Frank Mason North.

The Four Horsemen of the Apocalypse

FRANK A. TOBEY

☆ ☆ ☆ From the beginning of human history—even until now —the four horsemen of the Apocalypse have charged furiously up and down and across every land of this stricken world of ours. The rider of the "red horse" breathes out fire, destruction, and the horrors of war. The rider of the "pale horse" drops his mantle of death and carries off our loved ones frequently, at times and in places where least expected. The rider of the "black horse" kills our crops and defies man's endeavor to avert famine, until today one third of all humanity is subject to hunger and nakedness. But the rider of the "White horse" has received a crown; he carries a bow in his hand and he goes forth conquering and to conquer! He symbolizes life's conquering spirit!

In these confusing days in which we are destined to live, we must sadly admit that the white horse and his rider have been much less in evidence than the other three. In fact, during the last fifty years, the most conspicious has been the rider of the red horse of war.

Whether we like it or not, and we don't, this is the startling fact: "War has become the preoccupation of our time!"

In our lifetime we have experienced two world wars and since 1945 there have been at least two score so-called small wars. During the last half-century literally millions, yes, hundreds of millions, have been riding that fiery steed. And today we wait with baited breath, praying God Almighty to stay that red horse that prances so wildly behind the Iron and the Bamboo Curtain, chafing at the bit, pawing the ground, impatiently waiting for his rider to leap into the saddle to be off again into the fury of Armageddon!

We have been instructed, again and again, in no uncertain terms by the leaders of materialistic communism that we are their enemy, that we will be their victims, that they will bury us and destroy our freedoms. They seem to be in no hurry; they continue to dictate many world policies; their order of the day is a long campaign of attrition. Their greatest virtue is patience; they continually claim that time and history is on their side. They are pleased with the progress of their program to conquer the entire world, and well they might be. Theirs is the largest peacetime army in all history. Armed with modern weapons they advance insidiously whenever and wherever they find the opportunity. They threaten to conquer us by force, but presently they fear the consequences and as long as we remain strong they prefer to apply economic, psychological, and political pressure and to frighten us with their spectacular, technological advances.

To counter their military threat the leaders of the free world have deemed it necessary to maintain a high state of defensive military readiness. We have kept powerful forces deployed overseas for long periods of time. We have sent the youth of our nation to many remote and strange places in order to protect the periphery of the free world.

Yes, the long months of watchful waiting, the necessity for constant vigilance, the boredom and monotony of continued training, the lonesomeness and strain of being far away from one's loved ones while serving in distant lands create numerous problems that we, the chaplains, who always accompany their troops, are continually endeavoring to solve. I seriously doubt that the average American fully realizes or appreciates the tremendous sacrifices our young people still are making while they protect today the passes through which the ruthless rider of the red horse would charge if he could but catch us off guard.

But the rider of the red horse races not alone, for another rider follows in his wake. The rider of the black horse of spiritual famine is trampling under foot many of our cherished beliefs, beliefs which have nourished our souls and strengthened our faith for generations. He would render meaningless our redemption. He even questions the existence of the soul and the reality of God! Today he creates a famine of the soul, the like of which has not been experienced in modern civilization. Many millions hold out to him their withered hands begging for bread and he gives them a stone.

His followers are rapidly increasing in number. In the year I was born, Lenin installed Bolshevism with seventeen followers. In 1917 Russia was conquered with forty thousand of his supporters. Now his party has control over approximately a billion people. From 1946 to 1955 they conquered territory at the rate of forty-four square miles an hour, twenty-four hours a day, and today their leaders cry, "There is no God; there is no immortality; there is no sanctity of the sabbath; Jesus was a blasphemer —he was worthy of death. Ha, Ha, that is *if* he ever lived!"

While flying on a Pan American flight from Manila to Honolulu the steward aboard the plane stated that, as a student, he was in Russia for two weeks one summer. He noted that people attended church unmolested. However, the attitude of those with whom he conversed was best typified by that of one young woman who regarded him in a sad sort of way and remarked with pity in her voice, "You *really* don't believe in God, do you?"

It was Nikita Khrushchev who said: "We remain atheists and we will do all we can to liberate a certain people from the charm of the religious opium that still exists." They cry, "Peace, Peace," but there is no peace. They are engaged in a worldwide revolution with the expressed purpose of conquering the minds of men and destroying their faith in God.

Bishop Dibelius of the Berlin Lutheran Council informed me, when I last saw him in that city, that in East Germany there is an unlimited propaganda program for annulling church membership. In order to become an officer in the Communist-controlled East German Army a man must first leave his church. He stated that soldiers in that army are forbidden to have Bibles in their possession and then Bishop Dibelius concluded our conference by saying, "Materialistic communism cannot succeed until it first destroys the Christian church."

Yes, the rider of the black horse of spiritual famine would starve the soul of man until he becomes inert and lifeless. Then the pale horse of death rides forth seeking to kill! He would destroy all moral restraint, ethical standards, habits of temperance, modesty, reverence, honesty, and faith. The red horse of war and the black horse of famine welcome him as to a bivouac. They nourish him and send him forth to conquer the minds of men and to destroy their souls! He rides in every land, proclaiming his materialistic interpretation of man's destiny. He banishes the very thought of God from education, from business, from social planning, from politics. He obscures the spiritual purpose of life until men conceive their destinies in strictly earthly terms and according to materialistic patterns.

It would seem that here in America the fruits of godlessness, the fruits of materialism, yes, the fruits of that greatest enemy of the church are nearing maturity. The home, the basic unit of society, is collapsing. Crime statistics are steadily increasing even though they have already reached the pinnacle of astonishing heights.

Communism, as we see it today, is materialism or godlessness in its most active, violent, and ruthless form. But were communism suddenly to disappear and materialism were to remain strong, then materialism, this greatest enemy of the church of Jesus Christ, would still be facing us and war would not cease to be the preoccupation of our time. Communism is not the whole army, but communism is that sector where the army is holding the front and where the real enemy, materialism, is advancing that front as the opportunity permits. If their army wins in this sector, then the war will be over and the principles, values, and freedoms that the Christian church embodies and communism denies will vanish and *we will have lost!* Should this happen, then, the wounds inflicted by the rider of the pale horse of death would prove fatal to civilization as we know it today.

But wait, Christian, all is not lost! God is still God! Right still holds the balance in the sacred scales of life. The Christian church has never remained dormant for long. She was conceived for conquest and born to conquer. Today we must depend not only on nuclear weapons, awe inspiring rockets, and our own mental acumen but upon the purposes and plans of Almighty God. That is what the President of these United States meant when he declared that "religious faith is the prime strength of our nation." Christianity can never be placed on the defensive, for when Christianity ceases to be on the offensive then it ceases to be Christianity. Jesus said: "I *will* build my church; and the gates of hell shall not prevail against it!"

This is the place and this is the time in world affairs for the rider of the white horse to resume his place of leadership, for us to follow him, and for this to become the preoccupation of our lives. But are we following him vigorously and victoriously? Where are the 100,000,000 in America that statistics indicate profess Christianity? Where is the spearhead of resistance among us who profess Jesus to be our Lord and Saviour? Let us be honest with ourselves. Do we give mere lip service to our Lord and God? Are we educating our youth so that they will be fired with zeal, faith, and concern willing to witness to the saving grace of our crucified Lord wherever and whenever he calls?

Have we fallen into the error of sugar-coating religion, dressing it up, giving it "the Twist" treatment in order to inveigle young people into our fellowship?

During the last four years I have traveled nearly 200,000 miles inspecting the army's religious program, counseling with our chaplains, visiting in many of the sensitive areas of the world, and listening to men and women unburden their heavy hearts. I am convinced that we are rapidly approaching a most critical era that will demand of every one of us not an easy dedication but a difficult one of sacrificial service. Many today are undergoing untold hardships because of their faith. Many thousands of Christians now languish behind prison walls and many, many more are suffering persecution for Christ's sake.

Emil J. Kapaun, one of my chaplains in Korea, assigned to the English Cavalry Regiment, was captured by the North Korean Communists on November 2, 1950, while I was but a few miles away. He died in a prison camp six months later. He held services for his fellow prisoners as often as possible even though his captors ordered him not to. His fellow prisoners tell us of his last service, the Easter before he died. In "soiled and ragged fatigues" he stood before his half-starved congregation in a prison compound. Of priestly vessels he had only a dented cup. The prayer book from which he read was borrowed from a soldier. The crude cross he held in his hand was fashioned from two black sticks found in the prison yard. Shortly after that service they came to take him away. He returned the borrowed prayer book and charged its owner to keep on saying his prayers. He said: "Don't let them make you stop." When he saw that his men around him were near the breaking point, even then he sought to comfort them with these words of farewell: "I'm going where I've always wanted to go, and when I get there I'll say a prayer for you all."

Today the body of Chaplain Kapaun is lost forever in a mass grave somewhere in North Korea, but his soul has fallen in step with the saints of yesterday who dared to live and die for God's tomorrow. Yes, all of Christianity's triumphal horsemen have been conscious of riding with a victorious leader. They were following the eternal Christ of whose ultimate victory they had not a shadow of doubt.

Today the challenge comes to you and to me; while there is yet time, leap into the saddle, grasp the bow, and ride into the fray with a conquering spirit, smiting sin, revealing truth, preaching the gospel of Jesus— mighty to save—riding victoriously, if necessary, through peril, toil, and pain until the spirit of paganism flees forever before the blazing banner of righteousness and love, and all men everywhere in freedom are encouraged to accept Jesus as Saviour, Lord, and King!

This Business of Churchgoing

JAMES T. CLELAND

☆ ☆ ☆ One of my colleagues asked me what I planned to preach about in the Pentagon Protestant Pulpit. When I told him that the Roman officer in the seventh chapter of Luke was the theme, he commented: "Do you know Fort Monroe in Virginia? For the sake of your sermon you should know that the church there is named 'The Chapel of the Centurion.'" Let us think together about that Roman officer who is remembered on one of our present-day military bases.

Here was a soldier, engaged in policing Palestine with a hundred men under his command, presumably a junior officer in the Jewish army of Herod Antipas, the tetrarch of Galilee. In the first century A.D., his job was one of the most arduous in the Roman Empire, because in that century Palestine caused Rome more worry than the rest of the empire rolled into one. The steady stubbornness of Rome collided with the sheer obstinacy of Jerusalem. There was an uncanny "cussedness" about each of them, because each held himself to be one of the "chosen people." On the one hand, the Jews claimed to be *the* people, because of what was written in the Old Testament. It's in the book! On the other hand, the Romans

184

claimed to be *the* people because of the facts of imperial history. Look at the historical record! Theological pride clashed with experiential confidence, theory with fact. Neither would yield to the other, beyond a jot or a tittle. You can guess the outcome. It is paralleled in an analogy from the physics classroom where a teacher asked this question: "What will happen when an irresistible force meets an immovable mass?" A student, distinguished by common sense rather than by scientific knowledge, answered: "There will be an inconceivable crash." There was an inconceivable crash in Roman-Jewish relations in A.D. 66. In four years Rome rolled over Palestine—slow, ponderous, inevitable. It planned no *blitz-krieg*. It moved with glacier-like thoroughness. Jerusalem fell.

In that situation, around A.D. 30, this centurion was stationed with his men on the shores of the Sea of Galilee at Capernaum. There, Roman soldier though he was, pledged to uphold the empire and the emperor as his primary loyalty, he built a synagogue for the Jews. Jesus paid that officer, in a foreign army of occupation, as high a compliment as he paid anyone: "I tell you, nowhere, even in Israel, have I found faith like this." (NEB.)

It is not in the Bible but I am going to assume that he attended the synagogue. It was not an uncommon occurrence for Gentiles to be present at the synagogue services. They were forbidden to enter the inner courts of the Temple on pain of death, but there was no such restriction on attendance at the synagogue. Why did he go? Let me suggest two valid reasons, valid for him and for us.

First, *he wanted to worship the God whom he had chosen as the most important fact in his life.*

There was probably no need for him to build a synagogue for political reasons. He was not a proconsul or a legate or a governor. He was only a centurion, a junior officer, a second lieutenant. But he evidently had a religious sense. What does that mean? He knew that he himself was not ultimate, not all important. He knew that there was a fact in the universe, other than himself, greater than himself; other than Rome, more lasting than Rome. He knew there was a Creator, over against himself, a creature. Therefore he was humble. So he looked around for a God to worship. And out of the varied and various gods of the first century he chose the God of the Jews. Why? We do not know, but we can guess. For one thing, that God was just. You remember the lines which Amos wrote about him back in the eighth century B.C.:

> Let justice roll down like waters,
>   and righteousness like an everflowing stream.
> (Amos 5:24 RSV.)

That would appeal to a Roman officer. The Romans had a slogan: *"Justitia fiat, ruat coelum."* That means: "Let justice be done even if the heavens fall down." Justice undergirded the empire. More than that, the God of the Jews was holy, that is, morally whole. When a man thought of him seriously, then a man was forced to examine his conduct in the light of the character of this God. Read Isaiah on that. The Lord God of the Jews was a different kind of deity from the celestial beings on Mount Olympus. (They might be fun to have afternoon tea with, or ambrosia and nectar. But one may hardly accuse them of being holy.) There was a third quality which appealed to this soldier: This Jewish God was merciful. The prophet Hosea had discovered that. He had discovered it in his own experience, from his unhappy marriage. Most men need mercy, for one reason or another.

So this soldier chose as his God the God of the Hebrews. He did not become a Jew. He joined the circle of Gentiles on the fringe of Judaism, who were known as "the God-fearers." They worshiped in the synagogue but not in the Temple.

Hasn't that been the case with many folks ever since the first century? They cannot accept everything in the Jewish-Christian tradition, but they are God-fearers. They find in that tradition something outside of themselves to which they willingly pay homage. They find Someone whom they come here to acknowledge. For they know that the most important fact in their lives is their view of the universe, the quality and character of that which is spelled G-O-D. The Jewish-Christian God is that fact for them. They accept the name which Jesus gave him: "Father." "Father" is a shortcut way of bringing together the justness of Amos, the holiness of Isaiah, and the mercy of Hosea. A father, a good father, is just, holy, and merciful. So they ally themselves with what the Jewish-Christian tradition proclaims, when they come, Sunday by Sunday, to chapel and recognize that kind of God as *the* God and as their God.

186

Can that be true for us? I think so. During the last years of the second world war, I was chaplain in a New England prep school. One evening at Chapel the Headmaster read a letter from an old boy, written on the battlefield. He had just buried a classmate. There was no chaplain at hand, so this officer did what he thought right and fitting. He repeated the school prayer and the school hymn and the Lord's Prayer. He buried his friend, he commended him to the care of God, from and within the beloved community as they both knew it best.

That is one reason for churchgoing: the opportunity to respect, to worship, the God who is the most worthwhile fact in life, who gives us dignity in our humility, by calling us his sons and his daughters.

There is a second reason why that centurion may have attended the synagogue he built: *to keep his spirit sensitive in the midst of a world that numbs the finer feelings.*

That would be a sound reason for our centurion. His was a profession which called for heroism, for cold courage. If you would understand the kind of job it was, ask any British soldier who was on the same assignment in Palestine between the first and second world wars. Yet it was a job that was often callous and brutalizing, one apt to lower the tone and produce inner discord. But this officer had a sensitiveness to the things of the spirit. He recognized another side to his nature. He wanted to keep a grip on the finer qualities, on the gentler virtues. Therefore, he attended the synagogue. Service in an army of occupation was not the ultimate. Policing the outpost of an empire was not the be-all and end-all of life. There was another realm, another kingdom, to which he owed allegiance, in which he wished to live, too. "For he loves our nation, and he built us our synagogue." (RSV.) Within the Jewish faith, he kept his spirit sensitive.

We, too, live in a world which has been morally ugly in many of its major emphases for over a generation. It is a world of moral chaos, ethical confusion, and spiritual perversion. Moreover, it is a world in which the armed forces seem ultimate for many of us. It is not easy for us to find our way about in the realm of ideals and values in this year of grace. Something which Mark Twain once wrote in his notebook is almost a parable of our times. He was in Germany in February, 1892, confined to bed, while an important debate was going on in the *Reichstag*. Here is what he jotted down:

Thirty days sick abed—full of interest—read the debates and get excited over them, though I don't understand. By reading keep in a state of excited ignorance. Like a blind man in a house afire—flounder around—immensely, but unintelligently, interested, don't know how I got in and can't find the way out but I am having a booming time all to myself.[1]

Doesn't that describe us? Here we are, fascinated in our heads and sick in our hearts, as we try to steer ourselves through the moral Strait of Messina, between the Scylla of Washington and the Charybdis of Moscow, while listening to the voices of Fulton Lewis, Jr., Walter Lippmann, and Mr. Khrushchev.

Perhaps, like the centurion, we should come to the chapel, our synagogue, to expose ourselves to the things which are "true, lovely and of good report," to remain sensitive to spiritual values in that kind of a world. For in that kind of a world we must live—*in* that world but not *of* it.

That is another good reason for churchgoing: to keep the spirit sensitive in the midst of a world that numbs the finer feelings.

So we come to church. We come not to accept unthinkingly everything said, not necessarily to identify ourselves completely with everything done. We come, first, to know, to respect, and maybe ultimately to worship the God revealed in the Jewish-Christian tradition, which is the stuff of the ideals and aspirations of our heritage. And we come, second, to keep the spirit sensitive to the things of the spirit, in a world of recurring darkness and unwearied cruelty. For these reasons we can echo the words of the psalmist: "I was glad when they said unto me, Let us go into the house of the Lord."

[1] Albert Bigelow Paine, ed. *Mark Twain's Notebook* (New York: Harper & Bros., Inc., 1933), p. 222.

THE CONTRIBUTORS

Chaplain (Major General) Ivan L. Bennett (retired): former Chief of Chaplains, United States Army; now with the American Bible Society.

Sir Cyril Black: Member of Parliament, London, England.

John C. Broger: Director, Directorate for Armed Forces Information and Education, Department of Defense.

Dr. James T. Cleland: Dean of the Chapel, Duke University, Durham, North Carolina.

Dr. Norman Cousins: Editor, *Saturday Review*.

Dr. George R. Davis: Pastor, National City Christian Church, Washington, D.C.

Rear Admiral J. Floyd Dreith: Chief of Chaplains, United States Navy.

Dr. Edward L. R. Elson: Pastor, National Presbyterian Church, Washington, D.C.

Dr. Billy Graham: Evangelist.

Dr. Richard Halverson: Pastor, Fourth Presbyterian Church, Washington, D.C.

Dr. Frederick Brown Harris: Chaplain, United States Senate.

The Honorable George E. C. Hayes: Professor of Law, Howard University, Washington, D.C.

The Honorable Brooks Hays: Arthur Vanderbilt Professor and Lecturer, Eagleton Institute of Politics, Rutgers University, New Jersey; former Special Assistant to the President; and former President of the Southern Baptist Convention.

Dr. Oswald C. J. Hoffmann: Director of Public Relations and Preacher, National Lutheran Hour, Missouri Synod, Lutheran Church.

Dr. Laton E. Holmgren: Overseas Department of American Bible Society.

Dr. E. Stanley Jones: Missionary; Evangelist; and Author.

The Honorable Walter H. Judd: Missionary; Physician; Lecturer; and former Congressman.

Bishop John Wesley Lord: Bishop of the Washington, D.C., Area of The Methodist Church.

The Rt. Rev. Henry I. Louttit: Episcopal Bishop of South Florida; Chairman, Armed Forces Division of the Protestant Episcopal Church; and former Chairman of the General Commission on Chaplains and Armed Forces Personnel.

Dr. James I. McCord: President, Princeton Theological Seminary, Princeton, New Jersey.

The Rev. Robert B. McNeil: Pastor, Bream Memorial Presbyterian Church, Charleston, West Virginia.

Dr. Charles Malik: Professor of Philosophy, American University, Beirut, Lebanon; former President of the General Assembly, United Nations; former Minister of Foreign Affairs of the Republic of Lebanon; former Ambassador of Lebanon in Washington.

The Rt. Rev. James A. Pike: Episcopal Bishop of California, San Francisco.

The Rev. Edward H. Pruden: Pastor, First Baptist Church, Washington, D.C.

Dr. Paul S. Rees: Pastor; Evangelist; Author; and Vice-President, World Vision, Inc., Pasadena, California.

The Rev. Canon S. M. Shoemaker: the late Rector, Calvary Episcopal Church, New York City; and Calvary Episcopal Church, Pittsburgh.

Dr. Joseph R. Sizoo: Dean of the Chapel and Professor of Religion, George Washington University, Washington, D.C.

Chaplain, Major General, Robert P. Taylor: Chief of Chaplains, United States Air Force.

Chaplain (Major General) Frank A. Tobey (retired): former Chief of Chaplains, United States Army; now at the Balboa Union Church, Balboa Heights, Canal Zone.

Dr. Elton Trueblood: Professor of Philosophy, Earlham College, Richmond, Indiana.